Helmuth Spaeter
PANZERKORPS GROSSDEUTSCHLAND

PANZERKORPS GROSSDEUTSCHLAND

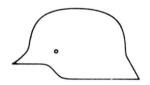

Panzergrenadier—Division—Grossdeutschland
Panzergrenadier—Division—Brandenburg
Führer—Grenadier—Division
Führer—Begleit—Division
Panzergrenadier—Division—Kurmark

including the 180 holders of the Knight's Cross

A Pictorial History

Helmuth Spaeter

Schiffer Publishing Ltd

1469 Morstein Road, West Chester, Pennsylvania 19380

In cooperation with the
Panzerkorps Grossdeutschland Tradition Association.

H.J. Krack
P.O. Box 1327
D-2330 Eckernförde

On the dust jacket:
German Zeltbahn (Soldiers shelter quarter/poncho), dated 1943
courtesy of the Military History Shop, Kennett Sq. PA.

Translated from the German by Dr. Edward Force,
Central Connecticut State University.

Printed in the United States of America.
ISBN: 0-88740-245-3

This book originally published under the title,
Panzerkorps Grossdeutschland Bilddokumentation,
by Podzun-Pallas Verlag, Friedberg 3 (Dorheim),
© 1984. ISBN: 3-7909-0214-4.

Published by Schiffer Publishing, Ltd.
1469 Morstein Road
West Chester, Pennsylvania 19380
Please write for a free catalog.
This book may be purchased from the publisher.
Please include $2.00 postage.
Try your bookstore first.

CONTENTS

FOREWORD

Three editions of the "Photo Album of the Panzergrenadier Division Grossdeutschland and their Sister Units" have appeared since 1970. Even the third edition has been out of print for some time. The constantly keen and—in other countries—considerable interest in photographic documentation of the battles of the GD units during the course of World War II have encouraged the publishers and the GD Tradition Association to consider a new edition. Setting the pattern for the new organization of documentation as presented here was the fact that in the thirteen years since the first appearance of the photo album, many hitherto unknown photographs and sources of information have been found. Our historian Helmuth Spaeter has organized these and the old materials anew, putting the emphasis on the battles of the years 1942 to 1945, in order to do a better job of portraying the "Sister Units" as well, which were treated in a more or less supportive manner before. Now all five divisions and the panzer corps which have borne the name of "Grossdeutschland" are described. This should say more for the colleagues (and their families) who wore the "Grossdeutschland" sleeve stripe only toward the end of the war.

In addition, the placing of this documentary emphasis affords the reader who is interested in the Panzerkorps GD a better overview of the sometimes scattered scenes of action where the individual Grossdeutschland units saw service toward the end of the war.

A list of bearers of the Knight's Cross who have been awarded the Knight's Cross or an additional decoration while in the GD completes this new edition, along with a full list of photo credits.

This volume is dedicated, as usual, to our comrades who fell in action—but it should also be a memorial to those who have been called to the Grand Army since then.

Many thanks to all who have contributed to this new edition—and most of all to our comrade Helmuth Spaeter.

Cologne, January 1984

Panzerkorps GD
Tradition Association

Peter Frantz, 1st Chairman

From Berlin Guard Command
to Panzerkorps GROSSDEUTSCHLAND

The Music Corps, its Chief Music Master Ahlers, and
the Drum Major (Sergeant Funk) of the Berlin Guard
Regiment in 1939.

```
Wachregiment GROSSDEUTSCHLAND

Im Zuge der Aufstellung der Reichswehr -
Frühjahr 1921 -      (lt.HV.-Bl. 1921) .. "Wachregiment Berlin "
19.Juni 1921 -       (lt.HV.-Bl. Nr.35 v.24.6.21) - aufgelöst
                     lt.Einspruch der li.-sozial.Reichstagsgruppe
Ende Juni 21/1922 (als Ausweg)     Kommando der Wachtruppe ,
                     unterstellt : Kommandantur Berlin -U.d.Linden
                     untergebracht ehem.Kasernen des
                     4.Garde-Rgt. zu Fuss und 1.Garde-Feld-Artil.
                     Rgt. Berlin  - Rathenower-Str.  -
                     Kp.-Bezeichnung: 1./ Wachtruppe Berlin
bis: 31.Aug.1934-                  : 2./ Wachtruppe Berlin
ab Herbst 1934 -     Umbenennung in :"Wachregiment Berlin " mit
                     Rgt.-Stab, jedoch keine Btl.-Stäbe.
ab: 1.10.1938 -      Aufstellung des "Wach-Btl.Wien"(lt.HV.-Bl.1938
                     Teil c v.15.6.38)-Kdr. Major Kandt,vormals
                     Kp.Chef 6./Wach-Rgt.Berlin.
6. April 1939 -      Befehl Ob.d.H. zur Umbenennung  des "Wach.Rgt.
                     Berlin" - in: Infanterieregiment GROSSDEUTSCHL
12. Juni 1939 -      (lt.HV.Bl. -Teil A, Blatt 7) "Wach-Rgt.Berlin"
                     führt mit sofortiger Wirkung:
                            "Infanterieregiment GROSSDEUTSCHLAND"
                     Kommandeur :Obstlt. von Stockhausen
Sept. 1 9 3 9 -      Restteile - etwa 100 Mann - in Berlin werden
                     in "Wach-Kp. Berlin" unter Hptm.v.Bölkow zu-
                     sammengefasst.
ab: 1. April 40-     "Wachbataillon Berlin "unter Führung Major
                     von Boguslawski
1.Oktober 1942 -     aus: "Wachbataillon Berlin " wird umbenannt
                     in:  "Wachbataillon GROSSDEUTSCHLAND".
1. August 1944 -     aus: "Wachbataillon GROSSDEUTSCHLAND" -
1. Oktober 44 -      wird: Wachregiment GROSSDEUTSCHLAND ".
ab: 27.1.1945 -      Abstellung von zwei Kp.'n zur Aufstellung des
                     "Feldwachregiment Hogrebe" ( Major Hogrebe)
1./2. Mai 45 -       Endkampf der " Kampfgruppe Lehnhoff in Berlin-
                     Schönhauser Allee .
```

Guard Duty at the Brandenburg Gate, Berlin, 1939.

12:00 Noon—The Guard Company, with musical accompaniment, marches through the Brandenburg Gate in Berlin.

They march past on Unter den Linden, in Berlin.

BERLIN—Rathenow Street—Garrison of the Guard Troop.

Döberitz-Elsgrund—Facilities of the Infantry Training Regiment.

Naming of the Infantry Regiment
GROSSDEUTSCHLAND, on Rathenow Street,
Berlin-Moabit.

Parade formation in front of the future garrison facility.

The City Commandant of Berlin, Lieutenant General
Seifert, inspects the men (July 14, 1939).

Training facilities for GD volunteers.

The City Theater in Cottbus.

Barracks for GD artillery, assault and heavy weapon volunteers in Guben, 1941.

Guben in flames—April 1945.

Neuruppin See-Kaserne.

In Neuruppin, in November of 1939, the "Infantry Replacement Battalion (motorized) 99" came into being; as of the beginning of 1940 it was to form the first training center for the GD.

Artillery training for GD volunteers.

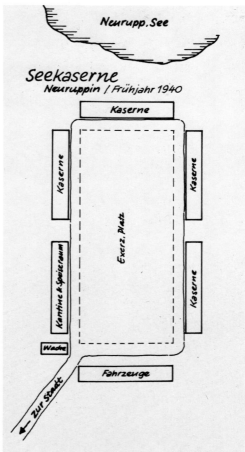

"Lake Garrison" facilities in Neuruppin.

The first Regimental Commander of the
I.R. GD, Colonel von Stockhausen.

GEFECHTSDATEN

des Leibregiments

1 9 3 9   des deutschen Volkes   1 9 4 2

1.10.39— 5.11.39 Verwendung im Heimatkriegsgebiet.

6.11.39— 9. 5.40 Verwendung im Operationsgebiet
der Westfront.

10. 5.40—12. 5.40 Vormarsch durch Luxemburg.
Durchbruch durch die südbelgischen Befestigungen und die Ardennen.
Vorfeldkämpfe an der Semois.

13. 5.40—14. 5.40 Erzwingung des Maasüberganges
bei Sedan und Durchbruch durch
die verlängerte Maginotlinie.
Durchbruch durch die Hauptkampflinie zwischen Frenois und
Wadelincourt.
Abwehr feindlicher Panzerangriffe bei Chemery und Bulson.

15. 5.40—17. 5.40 Kämpfe um die Höhen von
Stonne.

18. 5.40—21. 5.40 Durchbruch zum Meer und Bildung der Abwehrfront an der
Somme.

22. 5.40—26. 5.40 Einschließung der Feindkräfte in
Flandern und Erweiterung des
Durchbruches.
Kämpfe um Boulogne und Calais.
a) Gefecht bei Desvres 22. 5. 40;
b) Bildung von Brückenköpfen am
Aa-Kanal im Abschnitt St.
Momelin — Gravelines. Gewinnen der Brückenköpfe über
dem Aa-Kanal Holque, St.
Pierre-Brouck, St. Nicolas.

27. 5.40—28. 5.40 Angriff auf Wormhaudt und
Herzeele zur Einschließung von
Dünkirchen, Beschießung von
Dünkirchen.
Einnahme der Höhen von Crochte
und Pitgam.

29. 5.40— 4. 6.40 Kämpfe am Kanal de la Colme.
Kämpfe um Dünkirchen.
Einnahme von Bergues.

5. 6.40— 8. 6.40 Durchbruch aus dem Brückenkopf Amiens.

8. 6.40—10. 6.40 Verfolgungskämpfe bis zur Oise.

13. 6.40—14. 6.40 Durchbruch zur Seine.

15. 6.40—19. 6.40 Erzwingung des Überganges über
die Seine.
Erkämpfung von Brückenköpfen
an der Loire und am Allier und
Verfolgung über Lyon.

20. 6.40—25. 6.40 Sicherung und Bewachung der
Stadt Lyon.
Kämpfe gegen Isère und Westalpen.

26. 6.40— 4. 7.40 Besetzung Frankreichs im Verband der 12. Armee.
Sicherung der Demarkationslinie.

5. 7.40— 1. 4.41 Besatzungstruppe in Frankreich.

2. 4.41—13. 5.41 Einsatz in Jugoslawien.

5. 4.41—10. 4.41 Verlegung von Frankreich nach
Jugoslawien.

11. 4.41—12. 4.41 Gefechte um die Grenzbefestigung
Werschetz und Verfolgung bis
zur Donau.

13. 4.41 Besetzung von Belgrad.

14. 4.41—15. 5.41 Sicherung des ehemaligen jugoslawischen Raumes.

16. 5.41—27. 6.41 Verlegung von Jugoslawien nach
Deutschland und Generalgouvernement.

Seit dem 22. 6.41 befindet sich das Regiment im
Einsatz gegen den Weltfeind an
vorderster Front im Entscheidungskampf für Führer und Reich.

Preview of active service in the East.

15

With 400 men of the III. Battalion/I.R. GD under Lieutenant Colonel Garski, 100 Fieseler 156 A 1 Storks of the "Förster Group" take off about 5:30 A.M. on May 10, 1940, from Bitburg and Deckendorf airfields, headed for Belgium—destinations: Nives and Witry.

Fieseler Stork 156 A + C 1.

Pilot and crew of the Fieseler Stork 156 C 1.

"Nothing works without food . . ."

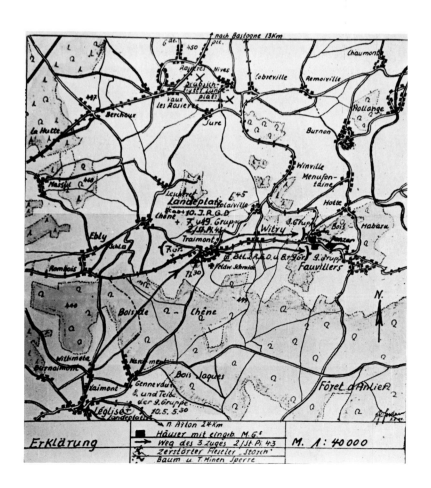

17

"Border fortress opened—open road to the west . . ."

The machine gun troop leads
the way . . .

Boundary marker: France . . .

The steady advance . . .

19

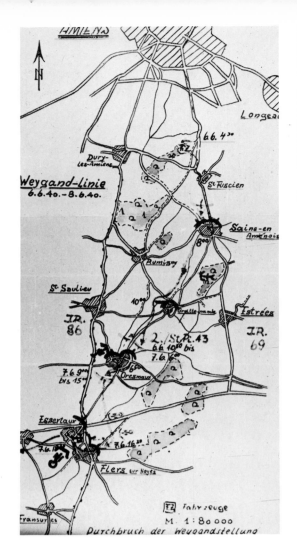

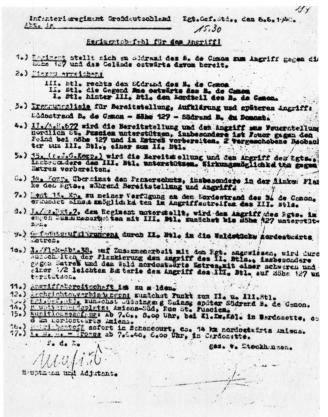

Regimental orders of June 6, 1940 to break through the Weygand Line to the south.

The first bearers of the Knight's Cross, First Lieutenant Beck-Broichsitter and Master Sergeant Hindelang.

The Regimental Leader of I.R. GD, Lieutenant Colonel von Schwerin, leads from the front.

Sergeant von Schirach with his comrades of the 12th Company/I.R. GD.

Short assault gun of the 16th (Assault Gun)/I.R. GD at rest.

Even railroad tracks are no barrier.

Motor vehicles advance— passing refugees' wagons on the road . . .

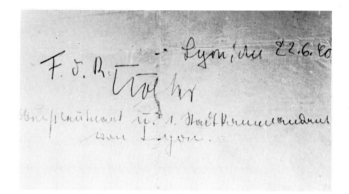

The destination—Lyon—is attained, the first City Commander, Lieutenant Colonel Köhler, I.R. GD.

The troops in their barracks "Le Valdahon" (January 27, 1941).

I./Infantry Regiment "Grossdeutschland"

Route of march on 4/8/1951: 5:30 A.M. departure Kittsee—Oroszwar—Ung.Altenburg-Raab—Komarow—Szöny—Dunaalmas-Nyerges Ujfalu—Dorog—Budapest-Alsonemedi—Keczkemet (250 km).

Route of March on 4/9/1941: 5:30 A.M. Keczkemet—Kiscun—Felegyhaza—Bzeged-Wagysentmiklos—Nemet—Perjamos Hanlik-falva—Ujarad—Vinga—Temesvar (220 km).

Note than on the Hungarian national territory
1. One drives to the left,
2. Clock time is one hour different from German summer time.

Transfer to Yugoslavia, motorized march through Hungary.

Hungarian police direct traffic.

Whether it rains or snows—motorcycle gunners are always there!

24

Map of Belgrade and Pancevo.

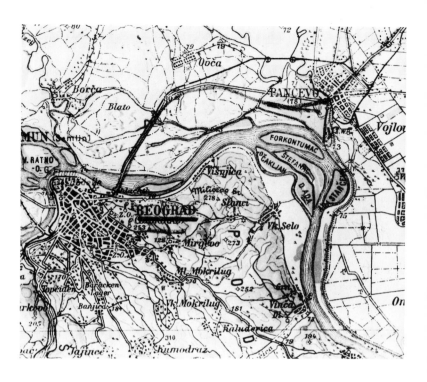

The bomb-damaged inner city—
Easter Sunday, April 13, 1941.

Rest stop—heavily dressed on
account of ice and coldness.

Medium anti-aircraft artillery defense installation at Pancevo.

The Lieutenant Colonel Garski Bridge at Konak, Yugoslavia, built by the 3rd Platoon/18th (Engineer) I.R. GD.

6/15-6/21/1941 Departure and taking positions for the eastern campaign.

Double battle of Bialystok and Minsk

6/22-6/24/1941 Breakthrough of the border position.
6/24-7/02/1941 Battle of Bialystok-Slonim.
7/02-7/05/1941 Advance against and through "Swislotsch" and "Beresina."
7/05-7/09/1941 Battle on the Dniepr.

Battle of Smolensk

7/09-7/14/1941 Breakthrough of the Dniepr position.
7/14-7/20/1941 Conquest of Smolensk.
7/15-7/17/1941 Fighting at the Dniepr bridgehead.
7/18-7/23/1941 Breakthrough to the "Desna" position at Jelnja.

Defensive battle at Jelnja and Smolensk

7/24-7/26/1941 Defensive fighting on the Chomare.
7/27-8/05/1941 Defensive fighting near Jelnja.

The border gate to Poland on June 22, 1941.

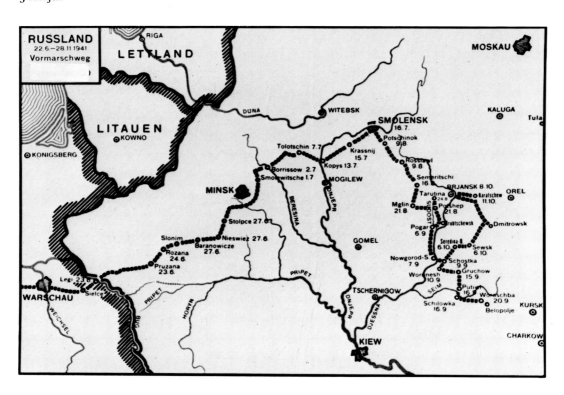

Route and action of "Panzer Unit 100", which accompanied the GD Regiment.

Heavy infantry guns and
tractors roll through a city in
the East.

The company chief explains the route
of march to his platoon leader.

Light AA guns—self-propelled—near
Dubrovka, June 1941.

Pontoon bridge over the Dniepr south of Sklov (photographed from the east side on July 12, 1941.

On July 11, 1941 the Inf. Reg. (mot.) **GROSSDEUTSCHLAND** forced a crossing of the Dniepr at this place—about 3 km south of Sklov, in the central sector of Russia. This picture was taken 24 hours after **the attack began on July 12, 1941,** at 5:15 A.M., from the bank formerly occupied by the Russians, and shows the attack lines of the I.R. GD. The first tank (P 4) of the 10th Armored Division is rolling over the pontoon bridge (Bridge Type B) built by the engineers, and pursuing the enemy.

On the other bank: Rubber boats, assault craft, bridge vehicles of Brüko B, tanks and vehicles of the panzer division are before the bridge, with the anti-aircraft position of the 20th (Fla) Company I.R. GD in the left background.

The length of the bridge over the Dniepr here is approximately 100 meters.

Report of "Spähtrupp Wolk" of the 6th Company/I.R. GD—late June 1941.

The Dniepr is conquered—a cigarette break for the 18th (Eng.)/I.R. GD.

Panzer Unit 100 crosses the Southeast near Pogar on September 6, 1941.

Launchers and heavy anti-aircraft guns as infantry support weapons.

8/06-8/22/1941   Defensive action in the Jelnja area.

8/18-8/30/1941   Defensive action on the Dessna.

Battle of Kiev

8/30-9/05/1941   Pursuit action as far as the Dessna. Break into the Dessna position. Surrounding of enemy forces in the Gomel area.

9/06-9/09/1941   Pursuit action in the battle of Kiev. Battle at Konotop, Romny and Lochwiza.

Colonel Hoernlein (Regimental Commander as of August 10, 1941) discusses the situation with Lieutenant Colonel Gehrke and Major Gericke.

General Guderian decorates soldiers of I.R. GD.

Tanks ready for action near Shilovka.

31

2 cm self-propelled anti-aircraft guns
of the 20th (Fla.)/I.R. GD moving out.

Close combat record of Sergeant Emde of the I.R. GD.

Supply columns in deep snow in the East.

9/10-9/25/1941   Fighting around Putivl.

Double battle at Wjasma and Brjansk.

9/26-10/3/1941   Fighting east of Romny
10/7-10/10/1941   Preparation for the advance toward Moscow in the Roslavl area.
10/11-10/20/1941   Battle near Brjansk.

The first winter clothing has arrived.

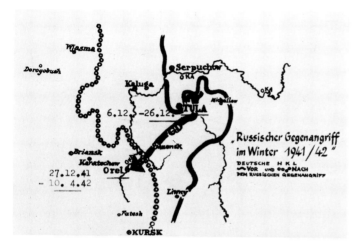

Colonel Hoernlein in conversation near Jagodnaja (January 20, 1942).

Machine-gun bullet traces in the snow.

Advance toward MOSCOW and WORONESH

10/20-10/24/1941   Fighting in the Jefremov and Tula area.
10/21-10/31/1941   Advance against Tula.
11/01/11/17/1941   Fighting around Jefremov and Tula.
11/18-12/05/1941   Battle around Tula and advance to Rjasan and Kashira.

Guns in open firing position.

Salute for the fallen Lieutenant Keiner near Bolchow in February of 1942.

The battle for MOSCOW

12/06-12/26/1941   Defensive fighting in the Jefremov and Tula area.

12/27/41-4/10/42   Defensive fighting north of Orel.

Retschitza—Rest and relaxation area for the reorganization of I.R. GD—April to June 1942.

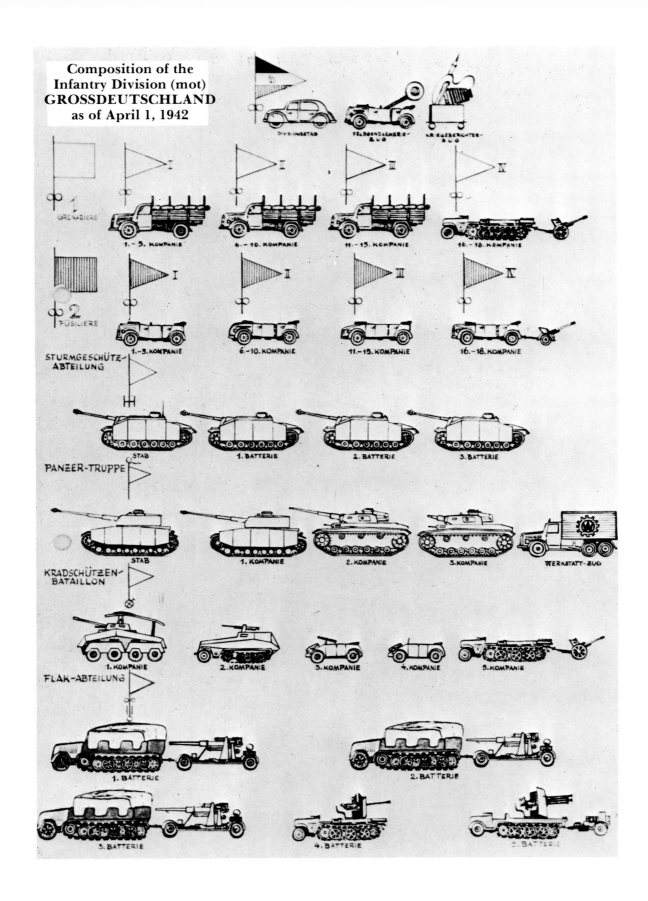

Composition of the
Infantry Division (mot)
GROSSDEUTSCHLAND
as of April 1, 1942

DIVISIONSSTAB FELDGENDARMERIE-ZUG AB KUEBERICHTER-ZUG

1 GRENADIERE

I — 1.–5. KOMPANIE   II — 6.–10. KOMPANIE   III — 11.–15. KOMPANIE   IV — 16.–18. KOMPANIE

2 FÜSILIERE

I — 1.–5. KOMPANIE   II — 6.–10. KOMPANIE   III — 11.–15. KOMPANIE   IV — 16.–18. KOMPANIE

STURMGESCHÜTZ-ABTEILUNG

STAB   1. BATTERIE   2. BATTERIE   3. BATTERIE

PANZER-TRUPPE

STAB   1. KOMPANIE   2. KOMPANIE   3. KOMPANIE   WERKSTATT-ZUG

KRADSCHÜTZEN-BATAILLON

1. KOMPANIE   2. KOMPANIE   3. KOMPANIE   4. KOMPANIE   5. KOMPANIE

FLAK-ABTEILUNG

1. BATTERIE   2. BATTERIE

3. BATTERIE   4. BATTERIE   5. BATTERIE

36

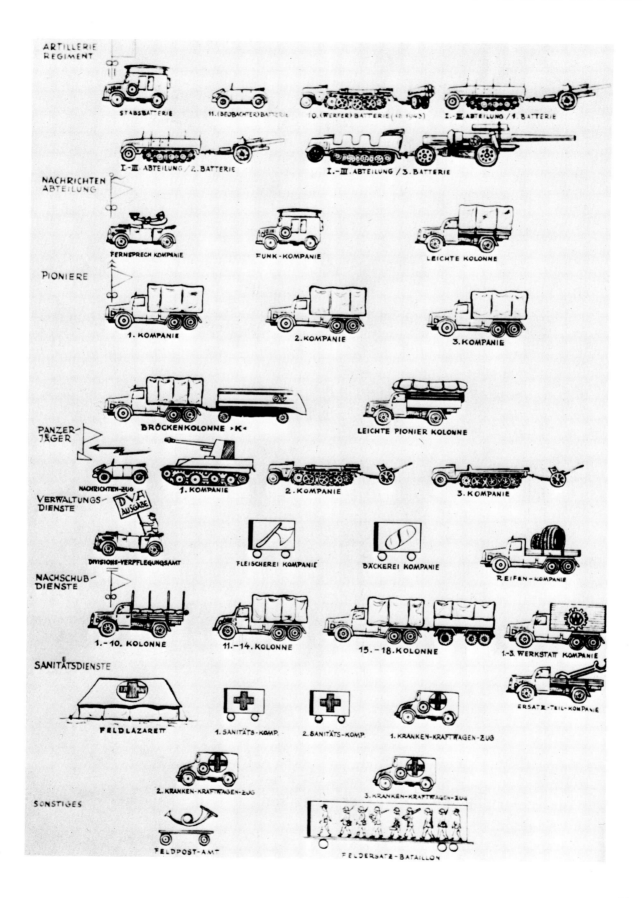

ARTILLERIE REGIMENT

STABSBATTERIE   11.(BEOBACHTER)BATTERIE   10.(WERFER)BATTERIE(12.1943)   I.-III.ABTEILUNG / 1.BATTERIE

I.-III.ABTEILUNG / 2.BATTERIE   I.-III.ABTEILUNG / 3.BATTERIE

NACHRICHTEN ABTEILUNG

FERNSPRECH KOMPANIE   FUNK-KOMPANIE   LEICHTE KOLONNE

PIONIERE

1.KOMPANIE   2.KOMPANIE   3.KOMPANIE

BRÜCKENKOLONNE ›K‹   LEICHTE PIONIER KOLONNE

PANZER JÄGER

NACHRICHTEN-ZUG   1.KOMPANIE   2.KOMPANIE   3.KOMPANIE

VERWALTUNGS-DIENSTE

DVA AUSGABE

DIVISIONS-VERPFLEGUNGSAMT   FLEISCHEREI KOMPANIE   BÄCKEREI KOMPANIE   REIFEN-KOMPANIE

NACHSCHUB-DIENSTE

1.-10.KOLONNE   11.-14.KOLONNE   15.-18.KOLONNE   1-3.WERKSTATT KOMPANIE

SANITÄTSDIENSTE

FELDLAZARETT   1.SANITÄTS-KOMP.   2.SANITÄTS-KOMP.   1.KRANKEN-KRAFTWAGEN-ZUG   ERSATZ-TEIL-KOMPANIE

2.KRANKEN-KRAFTWAGEN-ZUG   3.KRANKEN-KRAFTWAGEN-ZUG

SONSTIGES

FELDPOST-AMT   FELDERSATZ-BATAILLON

37

After reorganization it's now "Infantry Regiment GD 2."

Excerpts from the war diary of Motorcycle Battalion GD

4/01-5/23/1942 Establishment of the Motorcycle Battalion "GD" on the drill field at Wandern (Gross-Kirschbaum Camp).
5/24-5/29/1942 Transport by rail to Mielau (Mlava).
5/30-6/13/1942 March overland via Lomza—Bialystok—Baranowitze—Sluzk—Bobruisk-Rosslavl to the Fatesh area.
6/14/1942 March into the area east of Kursk.
6/15-6/24/1942 Camped around Sucherebrijk, east of Kursk.
6/25/1942 March to Denissovka.
6/26/1942 Camped at Dennisovka.
6/27/1942 March into the "Motorcycle Woods" near Novaya Alexandrovka.

Intelligence sergeants ready to go out.

The Gross-Kirschbaum Camp on the military drill fields at Wandern—May 1942.

Tactical emblems of Motorcycle
Battalion GD in 1942.

Major Binder, Commander of
Intelligence Unit GD.

Chief Field Surgeon Dr. Werthmann, Divisional
Surgeon, GD.

March route of I.D. GD to the south, toward the
Ukraine.

6/1-6/27/1942   Preparation in Army Group B zone.
6/28-7/20/1942   Breakthrough and pursuit to the Don, taking of Woronesh.
7/21-8/3/1942   Breakthrough and pursuit in the Donets Basin and toward the lower Don.
8/3-8/17/1942   OKH Reserve.

Road signs in Roslavl.

Railroad transport to Mielau (Mlava).

Radio Troop of the Motorcycle Battalion GD in the
Ukraine.

A Volkswagen in the mud.

Reconnoitering the country near Dennisovka on June
21, 1942. Major General Hoernlein, Major von Hobe,
Captain Bethke.

After night preparation—The attack begins, June 28, 1942—2:15 A.M. . . .

"Attack proceeds—Direction of the Don"—Units of the 2nd Battalion/I.R. GD 1 . . .

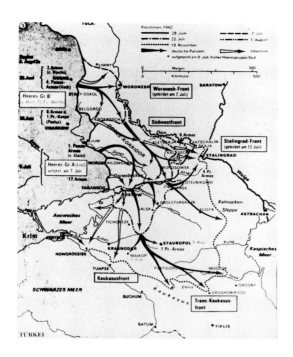

Dates of action as of June 1, 1942

6/1-6/27/1942 Preparation in Army Group B zone.

6/28-7/20/1942 Breakthrough and pursuit to the upper Don, taking of Woronesh. Breakthrough and pursuit to the central Don.

7/21-8/3/1942 Breakthrough and pursuit in the Donets Basin and toward the lower Don.

8/3-8/17-1942 OKH Reserve.

The upper map shows positions of army groups and fronts; the lower chart shows units of the Intelligence Platoon and Motorcycle Battalion of the Grossdeutschland Regiment as of June 26, 1942. The names under the vehicles are those of the unit commanders. The names at left: Advance Guard, Commander's Echelon, First Echelon Staff, Supply Train.

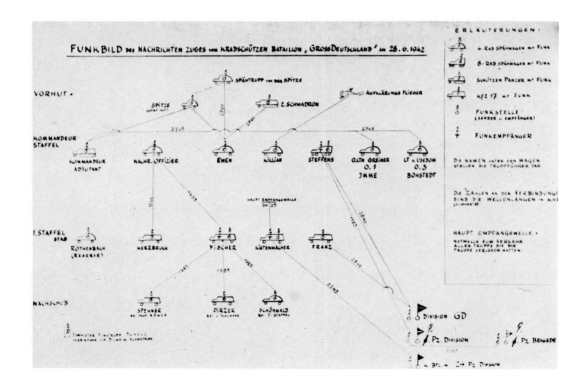

Wounded men and prisoners are cared for.

A halt in the march—at 40 degrees (Celsius) in the shade.

A destroyed enemy tank.

Lieutenant Colonels Köhler and Gehrke—Commanders in I.R. GD 1.

45

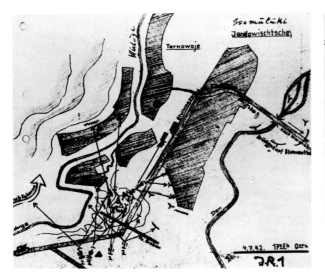

Freehand sketch: "First Lieutenant
Blumenthal's Exploit with the 7th
Company/I.R. GD 1."

Bridge units north of Woronesh.

Tanks on the march.

Infantry in place—artillery
moves up.

Russian prisoners are
moved back . . .

1st Battery/A.R. GD and their guns move forward—to the Don!

Tanks await action.

Again and again the infantry bears the brunt of the battle!

Planes report to tanks!

Stay alert while fighting for the town!

On the march southward—the 1st
Battery/A.R. GD with Battery Officer,
First Lieutenant Burchardi, Gun
Leader, Senior Corporal Posselt.

Soviet prisoners cross the line of
march—the artillery rolls and rolls.

The Gun Crew

Tractor driver

Aiming

Firing

Loading

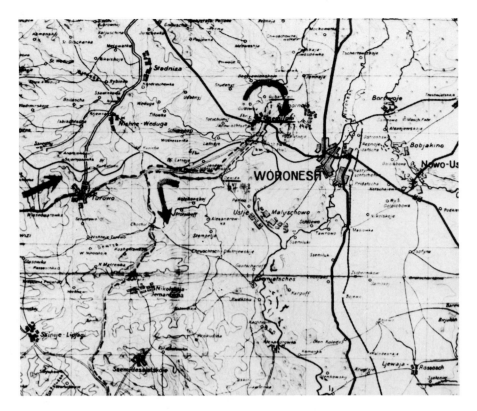

Making battle plans south of Woronesh, July 1942—present: General Hoernlein, his Ia, Major i.G. von Hobe, Colonel Reinicke and the ordnance officers.

At the head of the 3rd Company—the Chief . . .

. . . and his Group Leader in the Volkswagen.

Pontoon bridge over the Donets near Bronitzki—on July 18, 1942.

Our comrades remained behind on the route of advance . . .

In death all soldiers are equal . . .

GD grenadiers and Brandenburgers . . .

The 1st Battery in open firing position.

Fuel supply by air—a Ju 52 lands in an open field.

Recognition from the Division Commander, General Hoernlein.

The Don to the east of
Rostov is reached—
onward to the ferries.

Transport ferries near
Rasdorskaya—July 23 and
24, 1942.

Ferries at Rasdorskaya bring advance troops to the south shore of the Don . . .

Air protection of the bridgehead by 3.7 cm anti-aircraft guns of the GD.

Kalmucks from the steppes at the Manytsch . . .

Protection from tanks of the 2nd (SPW)/Motorcycle Battalion GD on the march to the Manytsch—the river forms the border between Europe and Asia.

Shipping records of the
2nd Battalion/I.R. GD 1—
on August 13, 1942.

Armored reconnaissance
on the way to the freight
stations.

The radio troop being transported by rail to the central sector . . .

Orel and Briansk—railroad stations on the edge of the transport area .

Road sign

Around Bjeloy

Dates of action as of August 18, 1942

8/18-8/25/1942 Reserve Army Group in Central Army Group zone.
8/26-9/9/1942 Army Reserve—A.O.K. 9.
9/10-10/8/1942 Defensive action in the Rshev area.
10/9-10/26/1942 OKH Reserve.
1Î5/42-1/10/43 Winter action around the block of the 9th Army (Modl).

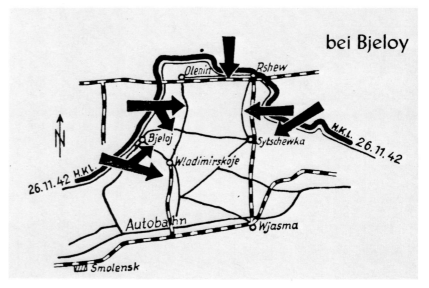

The Division Stork—Pilot Master Sergeant Wehner.

A truck in the mud near Subzov.

Living in a tent.

1st Battery/Anti-Aircraft Unit GD, with heavy tractors.

3.7 cm self-propelled anti-aircraft gun
—in the snow.

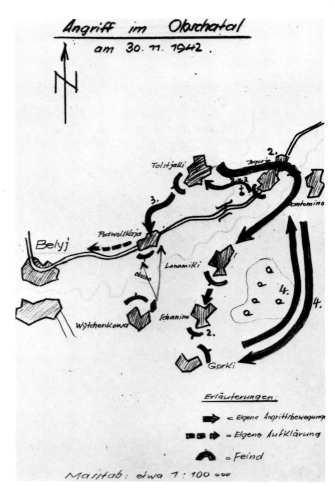

Attack in the Oloscha Valley

On November 30, 1942

Early deep snow in the Rshev area—an assault
gun on tracks, with its crew . . .

Fighting for positions in the Lutschessa Valley, southwest of Rshev.

A support point in the ice and snow—November 1942.

Observing the enemy from the hole in the snow.

Heavy infantry gun about to be fired.

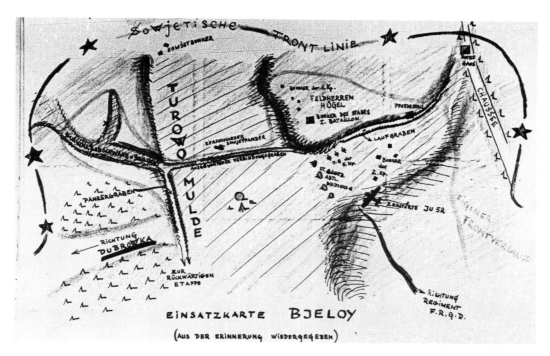

EINSATZKARTE BJELOY

(AUS DER ERINNERUNG WIEDERGEGEBEN)

Close combat record of Sergeant Dost, I.R. GD 2.

Map of action at Bjeloy
(drawn from memory)

On patrol through snow and scrub.

Bestätigte Nahkämpfe des Lt. D o s t .

```
 1. 12. 42   Ortsverteidigung in Wasnewo (Venice)
 2. 12. 42        "        "    "     "
 3. 12. 42   Angriff in Wasnewo auf Höhe 107
 8. 12. 42   Verteidigung und Angriff auf Höhe 101 u. 128
13. 12. 12   Angriff auf Höhe 123 und Alexandrowka
21. 12. 42   Angriff auf Schybinowk
25. 12. 42   Angriff auf Bugonow
27. 12. 42   Abwehr im Walde von Pisino
 4.  1. 43   Abwehr bei I. Btl. im Walde von Pisino
 6.  1. 43   Abwehr bei III. Btl. im Walde von Pisino
18.  1. 43   Vernichtung des Granatw. im Wald von Lubianka
 1.  2. 43   Angriff auf Michailowka
 3.  2. 43   Verteidigung und Gegenstoß in Michailowka
 9.  2. 43   Verteid. des Rgts.-Gefechtsstands Schebekino
11.  2. 43   Gegenstoß bei Ligzy
12.  2. 43   Gegenstoß auf Höhe 210
16.  2. 43   Durchboxen bei Kommuna
21.  2. 43      "       auf Medwesky
28.  7. 43   Minensuchen in Alechino
29.  7. 43   Verteidigung im Walde von Alechino
30.  7. 43   Gegenstoß auf Kastenwald Alechino
 1.  8. 43   Gegenstoß auf Alechino
 2.  8. 43   Gegenstoß auf Stellungssystem östlich Alechino
11.  8. 43   Säuberung und Gegenstoß auf Achtyrka
12.  8. 43   Säuberung und Gegenstoß auf Bachgrund Achtyrka
13.  8. 43   Angriff von Bachgrund auf Ziegelei Achtyrka
14.  8. 43   Gegenstoß auf Bachgrund Achtyrka im Rücken des Feindes
16.  8. 43   Gegenstoß auf Ziegelei Achtyrka
27.  8. 43   Angriff gegen Feind im Rücken III. Btl. bei Saitschens
10.  9. 43   Gegenstoß in Mulde Saitschens
 2. 10. 43   Gegenstoß auf Taranzoff
 7. 10. 43   Gegenstoß auf Ssokolowo Mulde
21. 10. 43   Gegenstoß auf Schlucht Didenkge
17. 11. 43   Abwehr in Lyubinowka
18. 11. 43        "       "
19. 11. 43   Gegenstoß bei II. Btl. auf Lynio
25. 11. 43   Angriff auf Metschinka
26. 11. 43   Abwehr in Metschinka
19. 12. 43   Abwehr nordwärts Wyssokyi
25. 12. 43   Abwehr und Gegenstoß in Wyssokyi
10.  1. 44   Gegenstoß auf Höhe 205,7
12.  1. 44        "       "     "   219
13.  1. 44        "       "     "   226
10.  8. 44   Waldkampf und Gegenstoß bei S. P. D. ########
16.  8. 44   Angriff auf Kurynai
17.  8. 44   Waldkampf bei 4. P. D. (Autze)
 9. 10. 44   Abwehr im Walde südwestl. Raguwiskiei
12. 10. 44   Gegenstoß im Walde südwestl. Raguwiskiei
```

Die Richtigkeit und Übereinstimmung der vorstehenden Angaben mit
dem Wehrstammblatt des Lt. D o s t wird hiermit bescheinigt:

Hauptmann u.

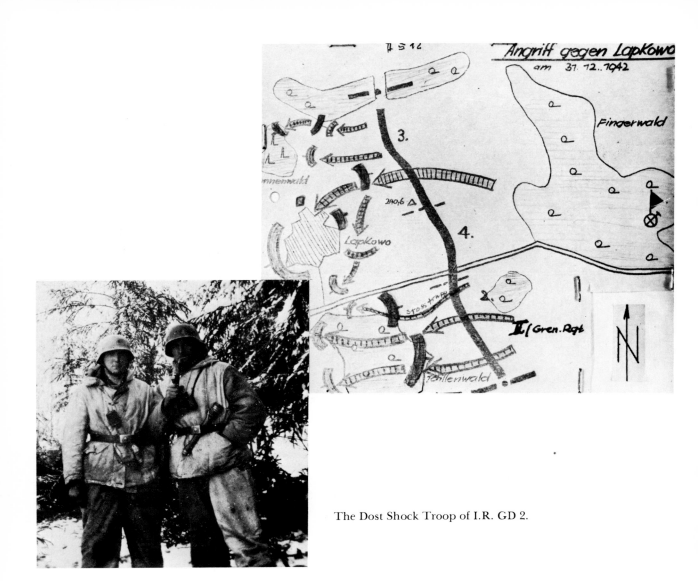

The Dost Shock Troop of I.R. GD 2.

Supplies come through a snowstorm.

Vieles ich dachte,   In euren Händen
Wenig vollbrachte,   Liegt das Vollenden,
Alles ich gab –   Mahnet dies Grab.

Diesen Vers schrieb im zweiten Weltkrieg ein junger Soldat kurz vor seinem Tod
einem Freund und Kameraden aufs Grab

Much I planned,
Little I completed,
All I gave—
In Your hands
Is the completion—
Remember this grave.

During World War II a young
soldier, just before his death,
wrote this verse on the grave of
a friend and comrade.

Soldiers' graves in the snow—
near Rshev.

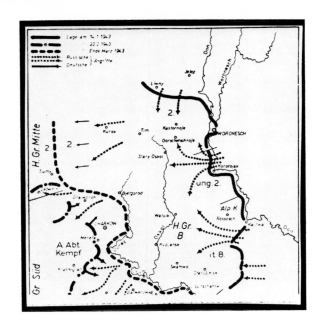

1/19-3/4/1943   Defensive action in the Kharkov area.
3/5-3/31/1943   Offensive action in the Kharkov area.
4/1-7/3/1943   Army reserve in the Kempf Army Department zone.

Assault guns on the march in winter—near Byelgorod.

Close combat record of
Captain Spaeter, Chief of the
2nd/Pz.A.A. GD.

Field kitchen supplies tank
crew during a lull in battle—
in the Kharkov area,
February 1943.

The first Tiger tank of the GD.

The road near Kharkov in winter.

3rd Battery/Assault Gun Unit GD on relay march.

Machine gunner II in winter.

Death . . .

. . . is the soldier's silent companion.

3.7 cm anti-aircraft gun in waiting position (badly damaged).

8.8 cm anti-aircraft gun in its winter position.

Light 10.5 cm armored howitzer 18 (SF) "Wasp"—in firing position.

Eight-wheel armored reconnaissance cars near Kharkov—February 1943.

Ready to attack—grenadiers and assault guns.

Soviet prisoners are searched.

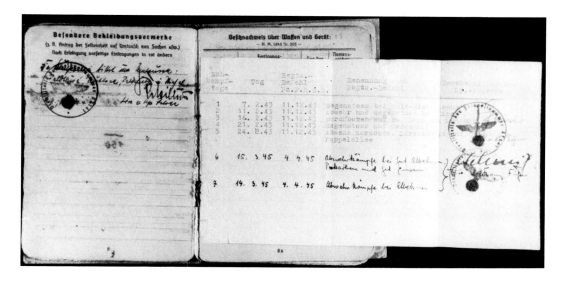

Assault record of
Sergeant Brondke of
the 11th/Füs.-Reg. GD

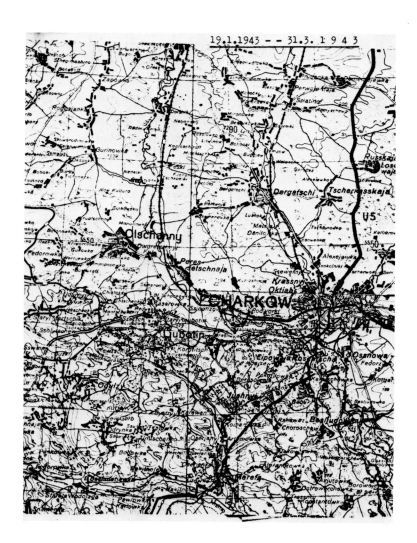

Map of the Kharkov
area.

Kharkov—Monument to the Ukrainian poet Schevtschenko.

3rd Battery/Assault Gun Unit GD in Kharkov.

Medical echelon in Kharkov on February 13, 1943.

Newspaper report of April 22, 1943 on the successful fighting in the Byelgorod-Kharkov area.

Division „Groß-|
vernichtete 838 (
PK. berichtet vom Kampf eines

757 Geschütze vernichtet
Stolze Erfolge im ersten Jahr des Einsatzes

Berlin, 22. April

Vor Jahresfrist wurde am Geburtstag des Führers das aus Freiwilligen aller deutschen Gaue gebildete Infanterieregiment „Großdeutschland" auf Grund seiner vorausgegangenen eindrucksvollen Waffentaten zur vollmotorisierten Division erweitert. Im ersten Jahre ihres Bestehens stand die von Eichenlaubträger Generalleutnant Hörnlein geführte Division immer wieder im Brennpunkt entscheidungsschwerer Kämpfe und rechtfertigte von neuem durch hervorragende Leistungen ihre Sonderstellung innerhalb der Wehrmacht.

Picture without words—the winter is merciless.

79

Road sign I b—supplies for the Poltava area.

Vehicle repairs by rail in the rest and recreation area of the Infantry Division (motorized) Grossdeutschland!

Outdoor tank repairs . . .

. . . with heavy lifting tackle.

A new weapon for the 2nd
Unit/Panzer Artillery
Regiment GD.

Drill with self-propelled guns
in May of 1943, 10.5 cm light
field howitzer 18 (Sf) "Wasp."

Modern battle equipment of the 2nd Unit/Panzer Artillery Regiment GD.

On June 23, 1943 the unit is renamed "Panzergrenadier—Division GROSSDEUTSCHLAND."

Heavy 15 cm armored howitzer 18/1 (Sf)—"Tomboy."

OPERATION "CITADEL"

7/4-7/12/1943   Offensive action in the Kursk area.
7/13-7/17/1943   Defensive action around Kharkov.
7/18-8/5/1943   Defensive action in the Orel-Briansk area.
8/6-9/14/1943   Defensive action in the area west of Kharkov.

Map—
Left:
Army Group Center
Army Group South

Right:
Soviet Central Front
Soviet Woronesh Front

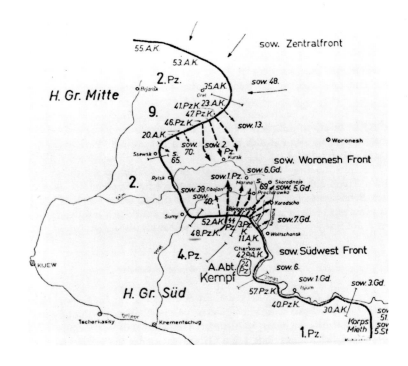

Generaloberst Hoth

Gliederung beim „Unternehmen Zitadelle"
— hier nur Angriffstruppen —

Nordteil der Front: AOK 9 (Generaloberst Model)
[Aufstellung von links nach rechts:]
XXIII. AK. mit 78. Sturm-, 216., 383. ID.;
XXXXI. PK. mit 18. PD., 86., 292. ID., 10. Pz.Gren.D.;
XXXXVII. PK. mit 6. ID., 2., 4., 9., 20. PD.;
XXXXVI. PK. mit 7., 31., 102., 258. ID.;
XX. AK. mit 45., 72., 137., 251. ID.;
Reserven: 12. PD., 36. Pz.Gren.D.

Südteil der Front: Pz.OAK 4 (Generaloberst Hoth)
[Aufstellung von links nach rechts:]
LII. AK. mit 57., 255., 332. ID.;
XXXXVIII. PK. mit 3., 11.PD., Pz.Gren.D. „Großdeutschl."
II. SS-PK. mit SS-PD. „A.Hitler", „Reich",
„Totenkopf".

Schutz der Ostflanke: Armee-Abt. K. (General d. Pz.Truppen Kempff)
[Aufstellung von links nach rechts:]
III. PK. mit 6., 7., 19. PD., 168., 198. ID.;
XI. AK. mit 106., 320. ID.;
Reserven: XXIV. PK. mit 17. PD., SS-PD.
„Wiking".

Senior General Hoth, Commander of the 4th Panzer Army.

July 4, 1943, the beginning of the unique major battle—"Operation Citadel."

Heavy 8.8 cm anti-aircraft guns as support weapons—loading and firing.

The heaviest fighting, booms and ditches—July 1943.

Panzer fusiliers in action in the forest bear Alechino—July 26, 1943.

Dug-in enemy tanks, once taken, offer cover.

Fighting in the forest near Alechino (July 26, 1943).

Great numbers of wounded men need their comrades' help.

A shot-down plane crew is taken prisoner.
Leader of a 7.5 cm antitank gun (Sf).

First Lieutenant Lex, 7th Company/Panzer Regiment GD, receives the Knight's Cross from the hand of the Division Commander on September 10, 1943.

A new type of tank, the "Panther", in action.

Close combat record of Corporal Wetzel of the 12th Company, Panzer Fusilier Regiment GD.

12. / Füs. Rgt. Grossdeutschland
Die Kompanie bestätigt dem
- . . W e t z e l , Erich
die Teilnahme an folgenden Nahkämpfen :

1. 4.7.43 Gwrzowka
2. 5.7.43 Beresowij
3. 6.7.43 Luchanewo
4. 7.7.43 Ol ychowaja-Schlucht
5. 8.7.43 Ssyrzewo
6. 9.7.43 Nowosselowka
7. lo.7.43 Höhe 258,5
8. 14.7.43 Nowosselowka
9. 15.7.43 "
1o. 16.7.43 "
11. 27.7.43 Alechino
12. 30.7.43 "
13. 12.8.43 Achtyrka
14. 13.8.43 "
15. 14.8.43 "
O.U., den 8.2.44

gez.
Leutnant

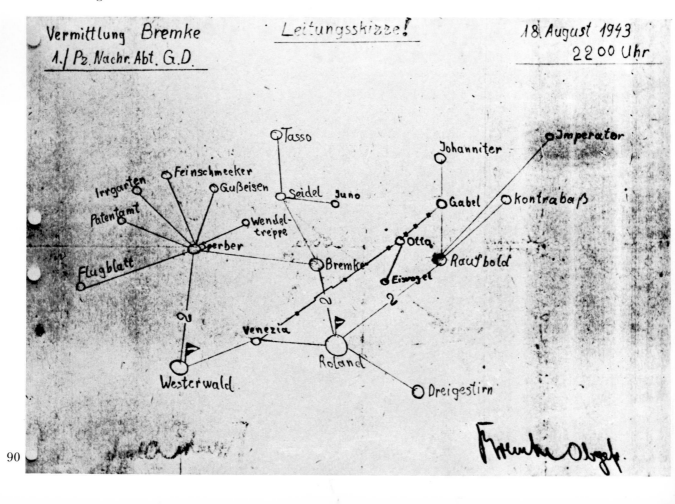

9/15-9/27/1943   Defensive action in southern Russia and retreat action to the Dniepr.
9/28-12/31/1943   Defensive action on the Dniepr.

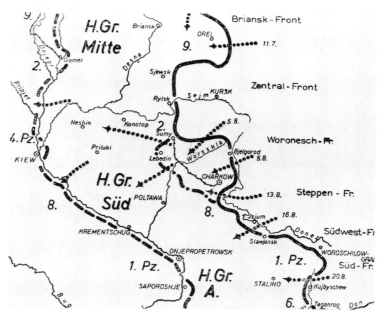

Retreat fighting through Sinkiev to Krementschug on the Dniepr.

Exhausted infantrymen after weeks of retreating.

Constand opposition from every ruined house.

Zero hour—dismount and march to the rear.

Assault guns with infantry escorts in retreat.

Surprise attacks with 2 cm light anti-aircraft guns (SFl) are effective.

Here too, the artillery is the backbone of the infantry.

Town fighting in Oposhnya—September 1943.

The "stovepipe", the grenadiers' heavy weapon.

Machine gunners fighting in a town.

Sergeant Karl Canje, 13th
Company, Panzer Fusilier
Regiment GD, badly beaten but
unbroken after six wounds.

Captain Kraussold, Battalion
Commander of Panzer Grenadier
Regiment GD, at Dikanka, 1943.

Retreat lines to the
Krementschug
bridgehead.

The leader of the shock troop of Panzer Fusilier Regiment GD, Master Sergeant Dost—in the Krivoj Rog sector—October 1943.

Two members of the Dost shock troop.

Group picture with Sergeant Poschusta, 2nd Company, Panzer Fusilier Regiment GD (Knight's Cross November 12, 1943—posthumously).

Enemy tanks advance—8.8 cm guns fire on them.

The action reserve of Panzergrenadier Regiment GD.

Wyssokij/Kirovgrad—December 1943.

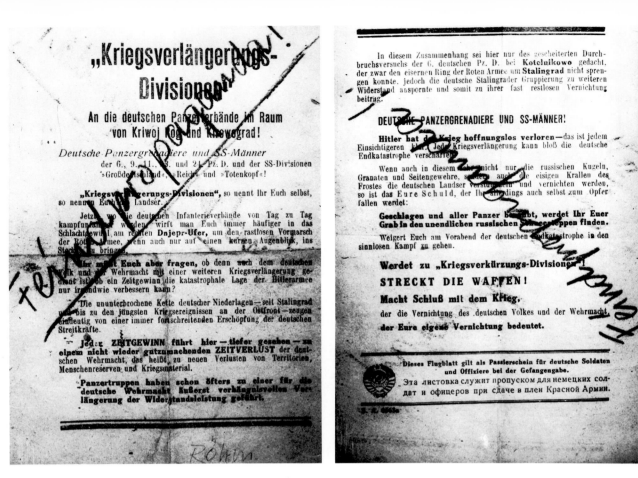

Enemy propaganda—and they keep trying it!

Light machine gun in position near Petrova Dolina/Krivoj Rog.

1/5/-1/18/1944 Defensive action around Kirovgrad.

1/19-3/6/1944 Fighting for positions on the lower Dniepr.

3/7-3/15/1944 Defensive action north of Nikolaiev and retreat action at the Bug.

3/16-3/26/1944 Use in rear zone of Army Group South during retreat fighting over the Bug and Dniestr.

3/27-4/25/1944 Defensive action in northern Bessarabia and the Carpathian foothills.

Stalindorf in Rumania.

Christmas Eve in Stalindorf.

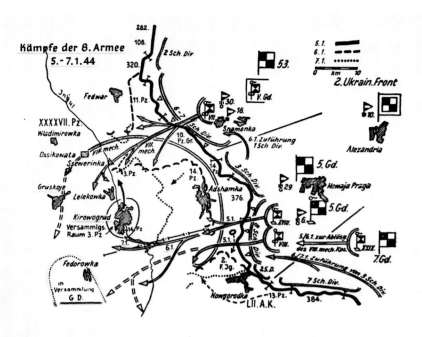

8. Armee   **5.–7. Januar 1944**

Map:
Battles of the 8th Army, January 5-7, 1944

Retreat south of Kirovgrad, as of January 4, 1944—Columns struggle through the snow.

Newspaper report of January 14, 1944: Not only successful defense--this report also shows the bitterness of the battle.

Erfolgreiche Abwehrkämpfe

Hohe Verluste der Sowjets in erbitterten Nahkämpfen

Berlin, 15. Januar

Im Raum südwestlich Dnjepropetrowsk versuchten die Sowjets kürzlich nach mehrstündigem Trommelfeuer ihrer Artillerie und Salvengeschütze mit neu herangeführten Divisionen unsere Stellungen zu durchbrechen. Im Abwehrfeuer aller Waffen und durch den entschlossenen Widerstand unserer Grenadiere und Füsiliere blieben alle Angriffe des Feindes erfolglos. Kleinere Einbrüche wurden in sofort angesetzten Gegenstoßen bereinigt. Die Bolschewisten ließen rund 2200 Mann an Toten und Verwundeten auf dem Schlachtfeld zurück. Außerdem büßten sie 14 Panzer, 13 Pak, 67 Maschinengewehre und zahllose Infanteriewaffen ein.

Als im Abschnitt einer Grenadier-Kompanie etwa 400 Sowjets in die deutsche Linie eingedrungen waren, warf sich ein Leutnant mit elf Grenadieren der feindlichen Uebermacht entgegen. Im Kampf Mann gegen Mann gelang es den Grenadieren, die Bolschewisten wieder zurückzuwerfen. Besonderen Schneid bewies hierbei der 19jährige Gefreite Kuhlmann, der als Kompaniemelder eingesetzt war. Obwohl er zu Beginn des Vorstoßes bereits verwundet wurde, stürmte er an der Spitze der kleinen Kampfgruppe weiter mit vor, vernichtete mit seiner Maschinenpistole allein über 30 Sowjets und erbeutete drei Maschinengewehre. Dem tapferen Gefreiten wurde

noch auf dem Gefechtsfeld das E.K. I. verliehen. Insgesamt verloren die Bolschewisten bei diesem Gegenstoß über 60 Tote.

Auch an einer anderen Stelle war es einer sowjetischen Kompanie von etwa 120 Mann gelungen, in die deutsche Hauptkampflinie einzudringen. Mit sieben Füsilieren ging der Oberfeldwebel Waldow gegen die Eindringlinge vor und konnte die entstandene Lücke hinter den eingebrochenen Bolschewisten wieder schließen. Während die damit abgeschnittenen Sowjets von Teilen einer Füsilierkompanie aufgerieben wurden, wobei 62 Gefangene in ihren Händen blieben, setzte der Oberfeldwebel mit Unterstützung von zwei Sturmgeschützen zum Gegenstoß gegen zwei weitere Kompanien des Feindes an, die den Eingeschlossenen zu Hilfe kommen wollten. Schon durch das Vernichtungsfeuer der deutschen Artillerie und der Sturmgeschütze erlitten die Bolschewisten hohe Verluste. Als die Reste der auf engstem Raum zusammengedrängten Kompanie durch den Feuerhagel der deutschen Grenadiere zu fliehen versuchten, stieß der Oberfeldwebel ihnen mit seinen sieben Füsilieren 800 Meter weit über die deutsche Hauptkampflinie hinaus nach und vernichtete sie im Nahkampf. Der kleine Stoßtrupp brachte 23 Gefangene ein und erbeutete 20 Maschinengewehre. Im Schutz der aufkommenden Nacht zogen sich die Füsiliere ohne Verluste auf ihre Stellungen zurück.

Wounds and frostbite—often only the divisional plane, the "Stork", can help.

The new GD Division Commander—Lieutenant General von Manteuffel—as of January 27, 1944.

Der Divisionskommandeur, General v. Manteuffel, in seinem Befehlspanzer

The former Division Commander, Lieutenant General Hoernlein, says farewell.

The "King Tiger" tank of the 3rd (Tiger) Unit/Panzer Regiment GD, in April of 1944.

A "King Tiger" with 8.8 cm gun and 12-cylinder Maybach motor.

From left to right: First Lieutenant Gerbener, Captain Diddens, Lieutenant Wenske—three officers of the time (May 1944).

3/27-4-25/1944   Defensive action in northern Bessarabia and the Carpathian foothills.
4/26-5/12/1944   Defensive action on the upper Moldau.
5/13-6/19/1944   Fighting for positions in the "Army Group South Ukraine" sector.
6/2-6/6/1944   Offensive action north of Jassy.

Anti-aircraft soldiers in ground action near Targul Frumos—May 1944.

Between actions—a quick pipe of tobacco.

Always watch the air—enemy planes in greatly superior numbers.

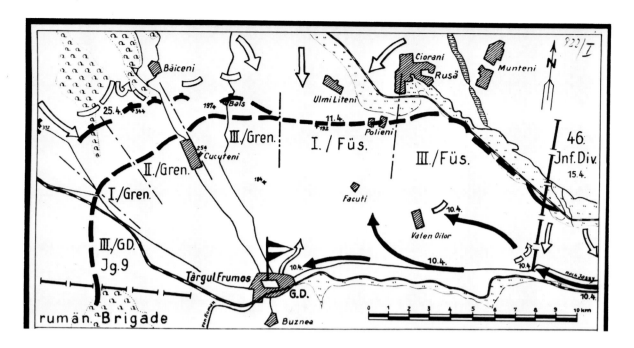

Map: Rumanian Brigade

Comrades-in-arms in 1944—Lieutenant General Manteuffel and a Rumanian officer.

Help your comrades!   Exhausted!

Time to pet kittens in wartime!

Grenadiers in retreat.

Resistance along the roadway.

Gilt als Passierschein !   Служит пропуском'

AN DIE SOLDATEN

der 2. Kp. des Pz.-Gr.-Rgt. der Division

„GROSSDEUTSCHLAND"

Vor einiger Zeit bekamt Ihr zur Auffüllung 10 Mann von der 4. Abtlg. des Art. Rgts. Eurer Division. Am 27. April kamen zu Euch die Obgefr. BEHREND und BÜHLEND, die Gefr. KORSCHNAK, ZALTEN, VOSS, SCHLÜTER und 6 weitere. And… …… …lle… Abteilung.

Keiner von ihnen hatte vorher bei der Infanterie gedient. Warum wurden sie jetzt bei der Infanterie eingesetzt ?

● **WEIL** HITLER keine Reserven mehr hat !
● **WEIL** HITLER es an Menschen mangelt !
● **WEIL** HITLER nicht mehr genügend Technik zur Verfügung steht !

Die großen Verluste an Geschützen, Panzern, Kraftfahrzeugen und anderem Kriegsmaterial, die die Deutschen während der letzten russischen Frühlingsoffensive davongetragen haben, ist Hitler nicht mehr imstande, aufzufüllen.

Die Artilleristen sind ohne Geschütze geblieben.

Enemy propaganda for the 2nd Company/Panzer Grenadier Regiment GD—June 1944.

Heavy tank losses for the Soviets too.

110

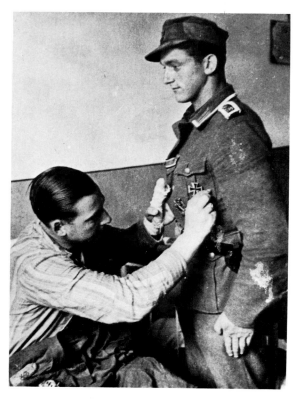

Sergeant Bludau is given the Iron Cross First Class in the hospital.

Fighting in an eastern town.

Regimental Commander Colonel Lorenz and Battalion Leader Captain Gerbener of Panzergrenadier Regiment GD—discussing the situation.

Again and again, fighting around every ruined house.

The frightened inhabitants seek shelter.

Tanks support the defensive action.

Having a quick bite to eat in Anti-Aircraft Unit GD.

Firing an 8.8 cm anti-aircraft gun at night.

"Barrel free"—Cannoneers clean their gun.

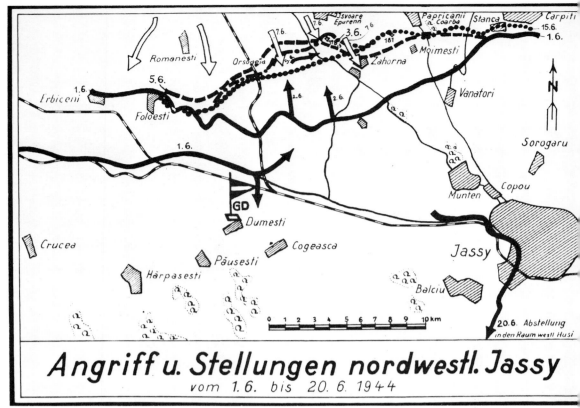

Angriff u. Stellungen nordwestl. Jassy
vom 1.6. bis 20.6. 1944

Attack and positions northwest of Jassy.

Lieutenant General von Manteuffel and his courier at Targul/Frumos—May 1944.

General Schmundt (Hitler's Adjutant), Colonel von Natzmer (1st General Staff Officer GD), Major Rochlitz, Commander of Anti-Aircraft Unit GD, at the fire control device.

Captain Petereit directs the Division Ia into the countryside.

Congratulations to Colonel von Natzmer on his birthday, June 29, 1944.

A tank commander gets ready for action.

Oak-leaf wearer Captain Diddens and his assault gun crew.

Observing the action—
The Division Ia and a
battalion commander.

The Division Commander at Captain von Wietersheim's command tank.

The GD front newspaper, "Die Feuerwehr" (Firefighters)—its first issue, June 1944.

⟨GD⟩ Die Feuerwehr

Grabenzeitung der Panzer- Grenadier- Division „Grossdeutschland"

| Nr. 1 | Erste Junifolge | 1944 |

Zum Geleit

Die „GD-Feuerwehr" will Euch Unterhaltung und damit Zerstreuung bieten sowie Anregungen und Belehrungen geben; sie will zugleich ein weiteres Bindeglied innerhalb der GD-Familie sein.

Auf dem Schlachtfeld hat uns das vorbildliche Zusammenwirken aller Waffen schoenste Erfolge gebracht, die ueber den Kampfauftrag der Division hinaus entscheidend waren. Der Gleichklang unseres Wollens wird uns unseren Herzenswunsch erfuellen: den Endsieg.

Heil unserem Fuehrer!
gez. von Manteuffel
Generalleutnant u. Div.-Kdr.

Deshalb kaempfen wir am Sereth!

D.F. Schaut auf die Karte Rumaeniens und Ihr werdet mit einem Blick erkennen, dass unsere Division die wichtigste Stellung dieser Front, das **Tor zum Balkan**, haelt: Überall bilden die Hoehenzuege der Vorkarpaten einen natuerlichen Schutzwall Rumaeniens nach Norden. Nur dort, wo die Fluesse — der Dnjestr, der Pruth und der Sereth ihren Weg zwischen den Bergen von Norden nach Sueden ins Schwarze Meer suchen, oeffnet sich das Land zu weiten Talmulden — den einzig gangbaren Toren nach Rumaenien hinein.

Wenn Ihr aber noch genauer hinseht, aus Eurem Graben dem Lauf der Eisenbahnen und Strassen nach Sueden folgt und Euch die Naehe des rumaenischen Erdoelgebietes vor Augen haltet und schliesslich bedenkt, dass an den Ufern des unteren Dnjestr — also suedostwaerts von uns — ebenfalls deutsche und rumaenische Kameraden stehen, dann wird Euch klar werden, dass wir hier zwischen Sereth und Pruth nicht nur irgendein beliebiges, sondern **das Tor Rumaeniens gegen die Sowjets** verteidigen.

Das haben die Sowjets genau so gut erkannt wie wir. Deshalb glaubten sie im April — unsere Absetzbewegungen ausnutzend — aus dem Schwung der Bewegung hier einen leichten und billigen Durchbruch erzwingen zu koennen. Dass es ihnen nicht gelang, dass sie von der Strasse Jassy-Targul Frumos wieder hinweggefegt und nach Norden zurueckgeworfen wurden, war eine entscheidende Tat unserer Division, die neben dem militaerischen Erfolg moralische Auswirkung auf die gesamte Front hatte.

Aber die Wichtigkeit, das Tor Rumaeniens am Sereth aufzustossen und die Hoffnungen, die die Sowjets damit verbanden — naemlich bis in das Kernland Rumaeniens ungehindert vorstossen und damit die deutsche Suedfront am Dnjestr aufrollen zu koennen — waren viel zu gross, als dass sich die Sowjets mit ihrer Niederlage abgefunden haetten. So massierte Marschall Konjew staerkste Panzer- und Infanteriekraefte (insgesamt 2 Panzerarmeen mit ca. 400 Panzer.

Fortsetzung Seite 2

In eigener Sache

D.F. Vor dem Richterforum der gesamten Division erscheint heute die „GD-Feuerwehr" und sagt — zur Wahrheit ermahnt — folgendes aus:

Zur Person: Ich heiss „Die Feuerwehr" und bin im Granatenhagel ostwaerts des rumaeinschen Sereth geboren. Ich bin das jeungste Kind einer geistigen Ehe. Meine Mutter hiess „Divisionsnachrichtenblatt"; sie ist allerdings sehr frueh verstorben. Mein geistiger Vater soll aus vornehmen „ritter"-lichen Kreisen stammen, aber er kuemmerte sich wenig um mich. (Der Feind nahm ihn, zu sehr in Anspruch.) Ein guter Vetter von mir war der „Karpaten-Kurier"; er starb eines ploetzlichen Todes auf der Reise zum Sereth, da ihm nicht nur die Luft, sondern auch das Papier ausging. So zur Waise geworden, nahm mich nunmehr der Kriegsberichter-Zug in seine verwandtschaftliche Obhut. Ich wurde „Feuerwehr" getauft, weil mir in die Wiege die Bestimmung gelegt wurde, den Wissensdurst anderer zu loeschen — und weil es auch sonst gut passt. Alte Leute wissen schon ...

Zur Sache: Wenn ich von nun an jede Woche einmal bis in das vorderste Panzerdeckungsloch komme, dann will ich nichts anderes sein, als Kamerad unter Kameraden. Nur fuer Euch und auch — von Euch. Denn: Jede gute Feuerwehr braucht ihren Motor, der Motor wiederum braucht Sprit, und so kann ich nur existieren...

> Wer graebt,
> hat mehr
> vom Leben

Lieutenant Thiel—War Correspondent Platoon GD— with a model of the front press truck.

8/6-10/4/1944
Offensive and defensive
action in East Prussia,
Lithuania and Latvia;
breakthrough to Army
Group North.
10/5-10/9/1944
Defensive action around
Triskiai and retreat fighting
to the city of Memel.
10/10-11/28/1944
Defensive and position
action at Memel bridge-
head.

Map shows positions of Army
Groups North and Center

Columns struggle northward—to East Prussia!

Events of the war in 1944 as seen in the press!

Infantry on the move in Lithuania—with Panther tanks of the 1st Unit/Panzer Regiment 26, subordinate to the GD— August 1944.

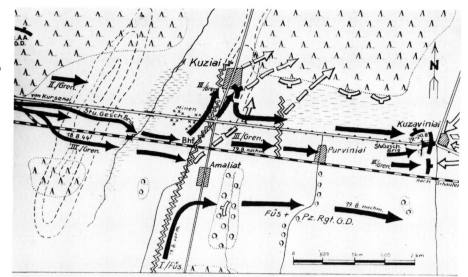

Advance of Panzer
Grenadier Division GD
against Kuziai and
Purviniai

August 18 to 20, 1944.

Stoß der Pz.Gren.Div. G.D. gegen Kuziai u. Purviniai
18. bis 20. August 1944

Panther tank of the 1st
Unit/Armored Regiment 26,
firing.

Soviet soldiers' graves
in Lithuania.

Preparations for an attack near Wirrballen—August 1944.

Digging in near Wirrballen—under tank protection.

Platoon leader in an armored car.

Team platoon for guns in the forest.

Colonel Niemack, Commander of Panzer
Fusilier Regiment GD.

The Tank Comander, Colonel Langkeit,
with Major von Basse and other officers near
Doblen-Mitau.

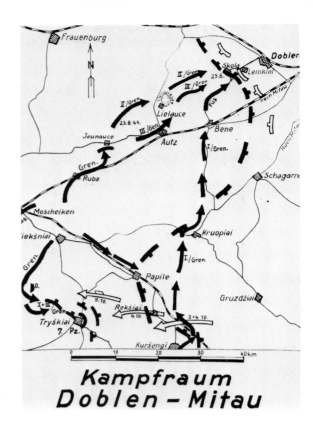

Kampfraum
Doblen – Mitau

Map: Battle zone Doblen-Mitau.

The results of the heaviest fighting . . .

Death and destruction.

Awarding the Knight's Cross to Sergeant Röger of Panzer Fusilier Regiment GD by Colonel Lorenz.

Captain von Basse and Sergeant Röger decorated with high honors.

Senior General Rauss, Commander of the 3rd Panzer Army, and Lieutenant General von Saucken, Commanding General of the XXXIX. Panzer Corps, in the Mitau area—September 1944.

The Division Commander GD, Lieutenant General von Manteuffel—with his soldiers.

The armored command car taking the Division Commander across the railroad bridge at Kursenai on October 4, 1944.

Soviet prisoners of war at Schaulen.

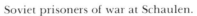

Officers of I./Panzergrenadier Regiment GD—October 6 to December 15 1944:

Battalion Leader — Captain Kuehn (Dietrich).

Adjutant — Lieutenant Bahndorf as of October 8.

Ordnance Officer — Sergeant Mrowinski.

Battalion Surgeon — Senior Surgeon Dr. Brodt.

Paymaster — Senior Paymaster Tapper.

Transport Officers — Lieut. (Eng.) Rejmont Ist Echelon Leader, Chief Works Master Liers.

1st Company — Leader Sgt. Zwillus, as of 10/10 First Lieut. Straihamer (in passing from Div. to Battalion Commander), as of 10/27 Lieut. Albietz, as of 12/1 First Lieut. von Prittwitz.

2nd Company — Leader Lieut. Bahndorf, as of 10/8 Lieut. Kollmitz, as of early December Lieut. Oster.

3rd Company — Leader First Lieut. Ochmann (Chief, on 11/17 transferred to 2nd Battalion), as of 11/17 First Lieut. Kristof, as of 12/17 First Lt. Jänecke.

4th Company — Chief First Lieut. Derben, as of 12/5 Leader First Lieut. Schmitt.

Supply Company — (Est. Dec.) Leader as of 12/4 Lieut. Bahndorf.

Pursuit Command — (Oct.-Nov.) Leader Sergeant Schabehorn (3rd Company).

Construction — (Oct.-Dec.) Master Sergeant Heuser. Officer

The Division Leader, Colonel Lorenz, talking with Colonel von Brese—in the area southwest of Mietau.

Colonel von Brese, Commander of anzer Fusilier Regiment GD, with the Regimental Adjutant, Captain Boll—September 1944.

Lage am 5.10.44
17⁰⁰Uhr

Situation on October 5, 1944, 17:00.

Major Hölzer, Commander of the 1st Unit, Panzer Artillery Regiment GD, in an amphibian Volkswagen on October 4, 1944—near Kurzenai.

Panzer VI - The "Tiger"
Weight: 69.8 tons.
Armament: 1 8.8 cm KwK-
L 71 and 3 machine guns.
Crew: 5 soldiers.

Loaded on railroad cars, camouflaged with bushes—the Heavy Panzer Unit GD—October 1944.

Tank V, Type A, the "Panther."

Weight: 44.8 tons
Armament: 1 7.5 cm KwK 42-L 70
Crew: 5 soldiers—Loaded on a railroad car, October 1944.

Paths of destruction—the Memel bridgehead

Major von Basse with group leaders—October 1944.

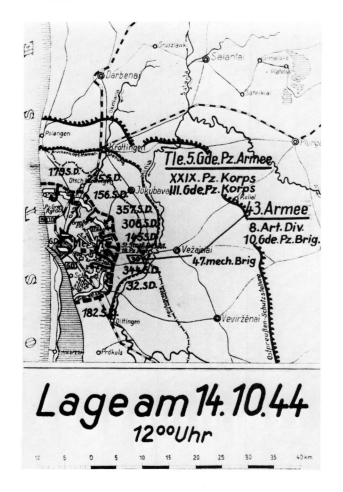

Enemy superiority before the Memel bridgehead—
October 14, 1944.

Heaviest fire.

German fighter planes bring relief near Windenberg-Rinten.

After an enemy bombing attack near Memel.

Refugees near Memel—October 1944.

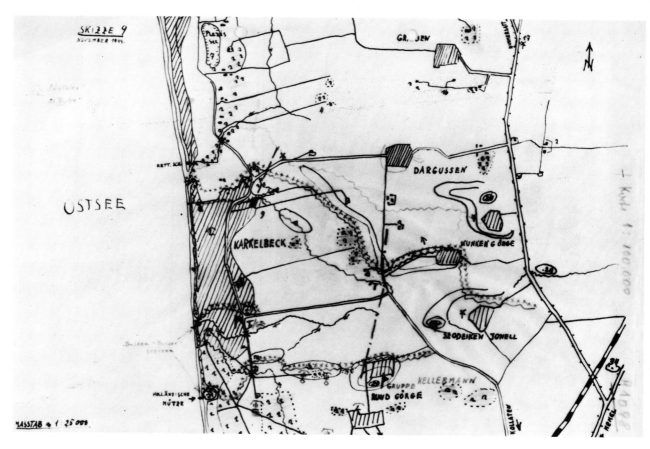

Hand-drawn sketch map of the battle area of parts of Panzer Fusilier Regiment GD near Karkelbek—November 20, 1944.

The coast of Samland west of Memel, with the 1st Unit/Panzer Artillery Regiment GD.

Graves along the paths of retreat.

Major von Werthern.

Panzergrenadier Brigade von Werthern—a battle group of Führer Escort Battalion GD.

On July 2, 1944 the Führer commanded the immediate establishment of the Panzergrenadier Brigade "von Werthern" on account of the Soviet breakthrough near Welikije Luki. Its formation took place promptly from the mass of the FBB and sections of the FFA. It was completed on July 5, 1944. Transportation from the Arys training camp in East Prussia to the front in the area east of Kovno took place on July 6, 1944.

The brigade's task was: To support the German divisions caught in heavy defensive fighting at their focal points in the Kovno—Wilkomir—Vilna area, and to hold back the Soviet fighting forces until a new defensive front was built up in East Prussia.

Major Frh. von Werthern

Nah-kampf-tage	Tag	Ort nach Regimentsbefehl	Bescheinigung
1 26	11.7.44	Gedraiciai	
2 27	12.7.44	Gedraiciai	
3 28	15.7.44	Aniksciai	
4 29	18.7.44	Upninkcliai	
5 30	19.7.44	Uzupes	
6 31	20.7.44	Kazlyne	
32			
33			

Farewell to the battle group at the Arys training camp.

Armored reconnaissance troop (four-wheeled)—ready to move out.

The Panzergrenadier Brigade "von Werthern" comprised two armored grenadier companies, one heavy company with anti-tank guns, heavy infantry guns—and heavy grenade launcher platoons, an anti-aircraft battery with 8.8 cm, 3.7 cm and 2 cm quadruple guns as well as one tank company with Tank IV and assault guns. There were also the necessary supply units. The complete strength of the brigade was approximately 4000 men.

The fully armored unit made its first contact with the enemy just shortly after its arrival in the Kovno area. It led to the brigade drawing the enemy action toward itself as a focal point in the following days. Thus it had very high losses during the entire Lithuanian action from July 6 to September 2, 1944. But the enemy also suffered very heavy losses in men and materiel.

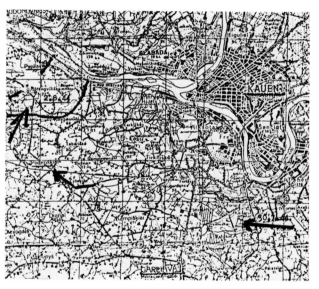

3-ton armored personnel carrier.

The Panzergrenadier Brigade "von Werthern" was relieved of its positions by other German units in mid-September 1944 after successfully fulfilling its task. On September 21, 1944 it was ordered transferred to the Arys training camp, the starting point of its action. The final disbanding of the brigade took place in Gross Stürlack, East Prussia on September 26, 1944.

It had fought bravely and gained repeated recognition for its achievements via the command positions, which changed according to the focal points of the defensive action.

Advance to Meissagola on July 9, 1944.

Observation in a suburb of Kauen.

Wounded men gather in a roadside ditch near Kauen.

Design for a tactical emblem of the FGB.

Colonel Kahler, the first commander of the brigade.

Transport train of the FGB.

Before that—Presentation in East Prussia.

Nachweis über Nahkampftage
A. H. M. 42 Nr. 1030

Gefr.
Teusch

Nah-kampf-tag	Tag 1944	Ort nach Regimentsbefehl	Bescheinigung des Kompanieführers
1.	24.10.	Gr. Jlbrode	
2.	25.10.		Jens u. Tp.-Fhr
	1945		
3.	10.1.	Trentelhof	
4.	11.1.	Trentelhof	
5.	2. 3.	Rachenau	Lt. u. Fhr.
6.	7. 3.	Schl. Neuss	d. Stabes
7.			

Close combat record of Corporal Teusch.

The brigade's first action in East Prussia—near Daken.

To the Ardennes offensive,
beginning on December
16, 1944.

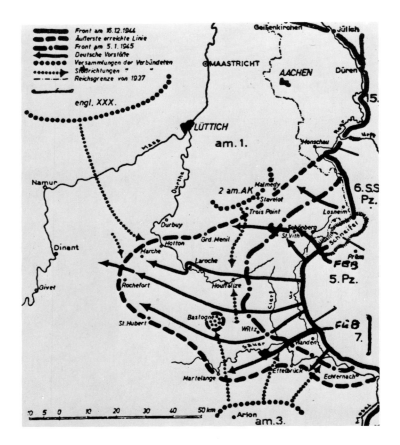

A tank commander,
wounded and burdened
with the weight of
responsibility (First
Lieutenant Kegel FBB,
1942).

Taken from the American side—Unsuccessful counterattack by parts of the FGB at Heiderscheid on December 26, 1944.

Emblems of the Allied troops—not only American but also tanks and Foreign Legion units of the French Army of Liberation—December 1944.

In the West too—mud and rain hinder the motorized units' movement.

Via Pomerania and Silesia to Vienna in April of 1945.

The Florisdorf Bridge in Vienna—last Danube crossing on April 13, 1945.

Last photo in May of 1945—Staff of the Führer—Grenadier—Division with Major General Mäder and his officers.

Into the lion's mouth—taken
from a magazine picture—
and looking impressive in
1944.

Die Führer-Begleit-Brigade
im Westen
1944-45

1 PRESSE NACHRICHTEN
2 LAGE - BARRACKE
3 FÜHRER-GÄSTE-BUNK.
4 BEGLEIT-KOMMANDO
5 BEGLEIT-KOMMANDO
6 STENOGRAPHEN BAR.
7 MARTIN BORMANN
8 HITLER-BUNKER
9 KÜCHE
10 TEE-HAUS
11 GÖRING-BUNKER
12 KEITEL
13 JODL
14 FRISEUR
15 ÄRZTE
16 NACHRICHTEN-BUNK.
17 GARAGEN
18 KINO
19 ALLGEMEINER BUNK.
20 BAHNHOF
21 KASINO
22 ALLGEMEINER BUNK.
23 STACHELDRAHT
24 EISENBAHN

NACH RASTENBURG   NACH LÖTZEN

First Lieutenant Kegel
of the 5th (Panzer)/FBB
in winter action.

Even during its formation, the Führer
Escort Brigade was moving to the West.

The white-painted tank of Lieutenant
Arnold of the 5th (Panzer) FBB.

A successful tank crew of the 5th (Panzer)/FBB.

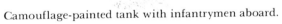

Camouflage-painted tank with infantrymen aboard.

Master Sergeant Scheunemann,
2nd/Panzer Regiment FBB.

First Lieutenant Geisberg,
5th/Panzer Regiment FBB.

Master Sergeant Scheunemann reports:

On December 23 and 24, 1944 I was ordered to an advance post with my platoon. If I remember correctly, it was the Motorcycle Unit of the Führer Escort Brigade.—
After a good advance on the road at first, the advance came to a stop. The cry "enemy tanks!" ahead—came through. On moving up to the front, I found that the other tanks had dropped out along the way—snow, ice, cold . . . Up front, an officer explained the situation to me. They had had quite a few losses from enemy tanks and were stopped by heavy enemy tanks.

Under enemy fire and without fire support, I went on ahead and could soon see two heavy enemy tanks that were shooting at us. After we fired at the enemy tanks a few times, one of them began to burn. After more shots, so did the other one. Then, under the cover of the burning tanks, I went on around them. The road was blocked by them.

At some distance I saw and heard—since we had shut off our motor—vehicle and tank movement. I opened fire at it. We alternated antitank and explosive grenades, firing at targets not clear to see. The enemy fire now decreased and soon stopped completely. Meanwhile the motorcycle gunners and one of our tanks had come forward.

Then I went on foot to the destroyed enemy tanks and trucks with the Leader and several men of the motorcycle platoon. I was very surprised to see so many enemy tanks with their motors running. After a short time the first crews of the enemy vehicles came out of the woods. They surrendered without opposition.

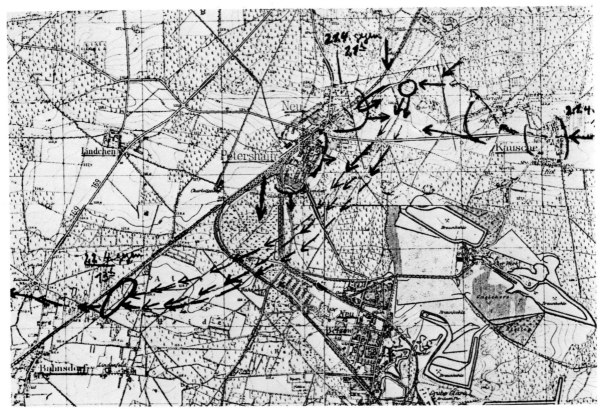

The downfall of the Führer Escort Division near Spremburg/Neu-Petershain on April 22, 1945.

The last gun in firing position.

Five GD Divisions—
their Commanders

General of the Panzer Troops von Saucken

General of the Artillery Jauer

Lieutenant General Hoernlein (GD)

Lieutenant General von Manteuffel (GD)

Major General Lorenz (GD)

Major General von Pfuhlstein (BR)

Major General Kühlwein (BR)

Major General Schulte-Heuthaus

Major General Remer (FBD)

Major General Mäder (FGD)

Major General Langkeit (KmK)

until 1/11/1945   OKH Reserve in East Prussia and northern Poland.

1/15-1/31/1945   Defensive action and retreat fighting in East Prussia.

2/1-3/12/1945   Attack to restore connections with Königsberg, defensive and position action in Ermland.

3/13-3/29/1945   Fighting in Ermland and retreat over the Frisches Haff.

3/30-4/12/1945   Army reserve in Samland.

4/13-4/30/1945   Defensive and retreat action in Samland and on the Frische Nehrung.

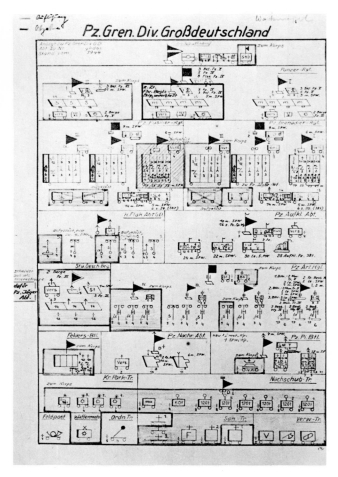

Another chart of the organization of the Panzergrenadier Division Grossdeutschland.

Encouraging news from the Commanding General of the "Panzerkorps Grossdeutschland", General of the Panzer Troops von Saucken.

Division fighting position GD at the railroad causeway of Wolittnick, East Prussia, on March 24, 1945.

The battlefield at Wolittnick.

Sergeant Larson of the
2nd/Panzer Regiment GD,
one of the most experienced
tank commanders, near
Palmnicken, East Prussia—
March 1945.

Division G.D.	P.P.Nr.	4720o
Rgt. Stab		o2736
I. Abt. Art. Rgt. m. G.D.		15158 A
II. Abt.		167o5 A
III. Abt.		32o82 A
IV. Abt.		14769 A
G.D. Feld Ers.Btl.		35915
Heeresflak.Abt.		o5211 A

2.Battr./ I.Abt./Pz.Art.Rgt. G.D.   1944 / Rumänien
                                            Jugoslavien
                                            Ungarn.
                                            Vasvui - b Bahu

6.	I.	1945	Feldtruppe
14.	I.	1945	Russ. Offensive beginnt
15.	I.	1945	Fraschnitz, Polen
19.	I.	1945	Wildenberg, Ostpreußen
2o.	I.	1945	Bartelsdorf
21.	I.	1945	Bischhofsburg
22.	I.	1945	Glockstein
24.	I.	1945	Ortelsburg
26.	I.	1945	Tiefensee (alles gesprengt)
28.	I.	1945	Kreuzburg
29.	I.	1945	Stellungsbau Tiefensee
31.	I.	1945	Pörschken
2.	II.	1945	bis
21.	II.	1945	in Brandenburg Haff, auch Zinten
21.	II.	1945	Großangriff auf Brandenburg
26.	II.	1945	bis
4.	III.	1945	Infantrie und Panzereinsatz b. Pervileken (Autobahn)
8.	III.	1945	zurück nach Gaffken
14.	III.	1945	Großoffensive auf Brandenburg (große Verluste 1o4 unserer Panzer abgeschossen, Nachtgefecht Panzer gegen Panzer
14.	III.	1945	Ludwigsort (Reparatur,neues Seitenvorgelege, neuer Panzermotor)
18.	III.	1945	Schoelen
19.	III.	1945	Renzegut (größte Verluste 1o8 gefallen, Rest 21 Mann)
23.	III.	1945	Kahlholz
27.	III.	1945	als letzte Batterie zurück auf Nehrung (Floßüberquerung, Balga Pillau) die letzten "WEIREN" gesprengt.
29.	III.	1945	in Pillau gelandet
3o.	III.	1945	Vormarsch auf Königsberg (Neuhäuser, Fischhausen, Germau)
31.	III.	1945	Rothenen erreicht
3.	IV.	1945	von Plinken nach Neukuren
12.	IV.	1945	HKL nach Rothenen zurückgenommen
13.	IV.	1945	vernichtender russ. Angriff beginnt im Samland
15.	IV.	1945	schlimmster Tag auf der Nehrung bei Neuhäuser, Russe schießt über das Haff - zurück bis Marinebefestigung Himmelreich Vorwerk Dammerow - Freies Deutschland beschießt uns direkt mit Schlagflieger (von Seydlitz)
21.	IV.	1945	Russe durch HKL (Kampf Mann gegen Mann)
24.	IV.	1945	Übersetzung nachts zur Mole im stärksten Feuer (Abwurf von brennendem Vosvor von 35.000 Mann erreichen 7.ooo das andere Ufer, Tote 15 Stück weise übereinander)
26.	IV.	1945	auf der Nehrung (bei km 4,5 am Russen vorbei durch die Ostsee bis km 14,2)
28.	IV.	1945	im direkten Panzerfeuer bis km 25,5 zurück
29.	IV.	1945	bis
3o.	IV.	1945	Infantriestellung km 29 mit Panzergrenadieren zurück bis km 47 bei Kalberg Verladung (von 224 G.Disten Rest 29)

Counterscarp—Gun positions on the Kahlholz Horn near Balga—March 1945.

Their faces express disappointment (March 27, 1945).

The steep coast at Balga, East
Prussia—March 27-28, 1945.

Rafts on the Haff near Balga.

Major General Lorenz gives last
instructions for transfer to Pillau.

Chronicles of the 2nd Battery/Panzer
Artillery Regiment GD.

Communication headquarters at Pillau,
March 29, 1945.

And if a few statistics can attest to the toughness of these battles, here they are.

Losses from 1/15/1945 to 3/29/1945 — 14,586 men, including 390 officers.
Losses from 3/13/1945 to 3/29/1945 — 5653 men, including 120 officers.
The 2nd Medical Company GD treated from 1/17/1945 to 3/28/1945 —6749 men.
The 1st Medical Company GD treated and transported from Kahlholz from
3/20/1945 to 3/29/1945 — 18,467 wounded, including 2392 unable to stand.

These statistics include GD men and men of other units—but all German soldiers!

The total losses of the Panzergrenadier Division GROSSDEUTSCHLAND alone
from January 15 1945, to April 22, 1945 — 16,988 soldiers of all ranks.

No one can count their wounds, nor measure their suffering, nor mitigate their
sacrifice!

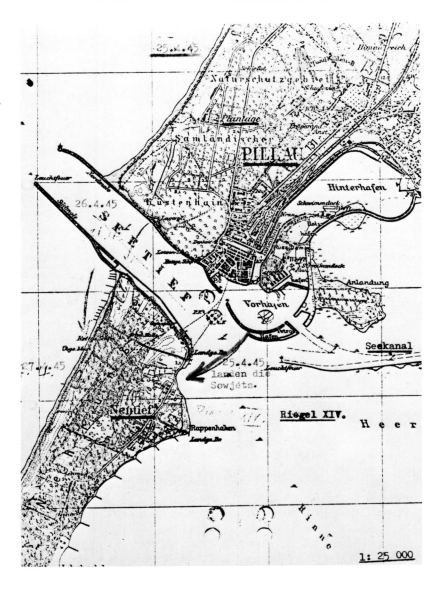

Last resistance of the last GD battle groups at Pillau, April 25-26, 1945.

The "sea snake" on its way to Pillau.

160

NACHRICHTENBLATT

für die deutsche Bevölkerung

Nr. 18   9. Mai 1945

Unterzeichnung der Urkunde über die bedingungslose Kapitulation der deutschen Streitkräfte

Urkunde über die militärische Kapitulation

1. Wir Endesunterzeichneten, die wir im Namen des deutschen Oberkommandos handeln, erklären die bedingungslose Kapitulation aller unserer Streitkräfte zu Lande, zu Wasser und in der Luft sowie aller übrigen Streitkräfte, die zur Zeit unter deutschem Befehl stehen, vor dem Oberkommando der Roten Armee und gleichzeitig vor dem Oberkommando der Alliierten Expeditionsstreitkräfte.

2. Das deutsche Oberkommando erteilt unverzüglich allen Befehlshabern des Heeres, der Marine und der Luftwaffe und allen von Deutschland beherrschten Streitkräften Befehl, die Kampfhandlungen am 8. Mai 1945 um 23.01 Uhr mitteleuropäischer Zeit einzustellen, in den Stellungen zu verbleiben, in denen sie sich zu dieser Zeit befinden, sich vollständig zu entwaffnen, indem sie alle Waffen und alles Kriegsgut den örtlichen Verbündeten Befehlshabern oder den durch die Vertreter des Verbündeten Oberkommandos bestimmten Offizieren abliefern, sowie Schiffe, Boote und Flugzeuge, ihre maschinellen Einrichtungen, Rümpfe und Ausstattungen, ferner Maschinen, Bewaffnung, Apparate und technische Gegenstände, die Kriegszwecken im allgemeinen dienstlich sein können, weder zu vernichten noch zu beschädigen.

Unterzeichnet am 8. Mai 1945 in Berlin.

3. Das deutsche Oberkommando bestimmt unverzüglich die entsprechenden Kommandeure und stellt die Durchführung aller weiteren vom Oberkommando der Roten Armee und dem Oberkommando der Alliierten Expeditionsstreitkräfte herausgegebenen Befehle sicher.

4. Diese Urkunde steht der Ersetzung durch ein anderes Generaldokument über die Kapitulation nicht im Wege, das von den Vereinten Nationen oder in deren Namen bezüglich Deutschlands und seiner Streitkräfte im ganzen abgeschlossen wird.

5. Sollten das deutsche Oberkommando oder irgendwelche Streitkräfte, die unter seinem Befehl stehen, nicht gemäß dieser Kapitulationsurkunde handeln, so werden das Oberkommando der Roten Armee ebenso wie das Oberkommando der Alliierten Expeditionsstreitkräfte diejenigen Strafmaßnahmen ergreifen oder andere Handlungen durchführen, die sie für notwendig erachten.

6. Diese Urkunde ist in russischer, englischer und deutscher Sprache ausgefertigt. Nur der russische und der englische Text sind authentisch.

Im Namen des deutschen Oberkommandos:
KEITEL, FRIEDEBURG, STUMPF

Es waren anwesend:

Im Auftrag des Oberkommandos der Roten Armee
Marschall der Sowjetunion
G. SHUKOW

Im Auftrag des Obersten Befehlshabers der Expeditionsstreitkräfte der Alliierten
Hauptmarschall der Luftstreitkräfte
TEDDER

Bei der Unterzeichnung waren als Zeugen anwesend:

Der Befehlshaber der strategischen Luftstreitkräfte der U.S.A.
General SPAATZ

Der Oberbefehlshaber der französischen Armee
General DELATRE DE TASSIGNY

ERLASS

des Präsidiums des Obersten Sowjets der UdSSR

9. Mai zum Feiertag des Sieges erklärt

Zu Ehren des siegreichen Abschlusses des Großen Vaterländischen Krieges des Sowjetvolkes gegen die deutschfaschistischen Eindringlinge und zu Ehren der von der Roten Armee errungenen historischen Siege, die durch die volle

Niederschlagung Hitlerdeutschlands, das seine bedingungslose Kapitulation erklärt hat, gekrönt wurden, wird festgesetzt, daß der 9. Mai ein Festtag des gesamten Volkes — der FEIERTAG DES SIEGES ist.

Der 9. Mai gilt als arbeitsfreier Tag.

Der Vorsitzende des Präsidiums des Obersten Sowjets der UdSSR
M. KALININ

Der Sekretär des Obersten Präsidiums der UdSSR
A. GORKIN

Moskau, Kreml, 8. Mai 1945.

May 9, 1945—
Announcement from
the Soviet forces.

Beaten troops—but
they are alive!

BRANDENBURG

Military High Command
Ausl.Abw. Office/Chief
No. 1509/42 g.Kdos/Abw.II/Chief   Berlin, June 26, 1942

Task of the Training Regiment "Brandenburg" z.b.V. 800 is battle-ready camouflaged action against tactical, operational or war-economy-important objectives. It is to take place where other units of the fighting forces have not yet been or are no longer able to fight.

In view of the significance of quick movements in modern warfare, the taking possession of transport facilities, particularly of bridges, is of prime importance. The special use of units of the Training Regiment "Brandenburg" z.b.V. 800 is to deceive the enemy through the use of military tricks of all kinds and thus take war-important objectives from him by surprise. Making full use of this special action tactically and operationally is the responsibility of the leadership of the following troops.

The first headquarters of Training Regiment BR zbV 800 in Berlin, Matthäi-Kirchplatz 5, in 1941.

Magedburger Strasse Barracks on Brandenburg on the Havel.

Freiburg in Breisgau, for the 1st Regiment BR.

Düren for the 2rd Regiment BR.

Weilburg/Baden, Austria for the 2nd Regiment BR.

2. Regiment "BR" z.b.V. 800

7th Company/LRB
advancing in Lithuania,
1941.

Motorcycle courier of the
Intelligence Unit BR.

Death and destruction on the advance route in the East—July 1941.

At the Enger-Abschnitt in 1941.

Hand-drawn sketch map of Ljudovka for the 2nd Company, Training Regiment BR zbV 800—on July 18, 1941.

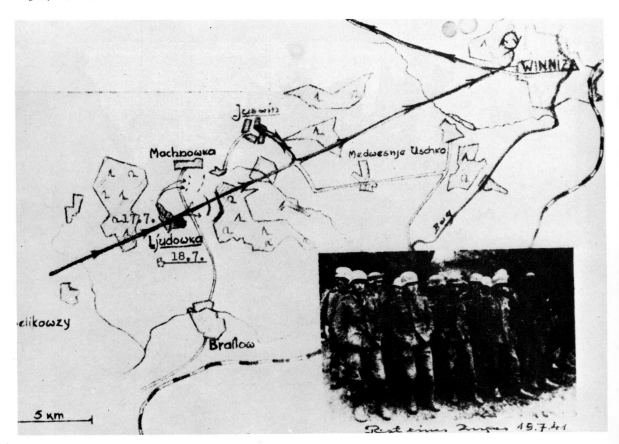

Radio contact—German and Finnish comrades.

A battle group of the Brandenburgers advancing on the corduroy road from Kiestinki, Finland in 1942.

In the South as in the North—here in Finland—Brandenburgers are in action—here the 15th(light) Company/Training Regiment BR zbV 800.

Nachrichten-Verbände z.b.V. 800

The bridge at Bataisk—August 1942.

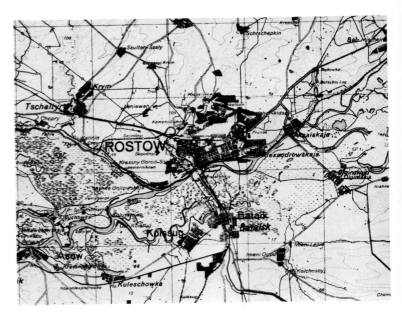

Later: The railroad
station at Bataisk,
south of Rostov.

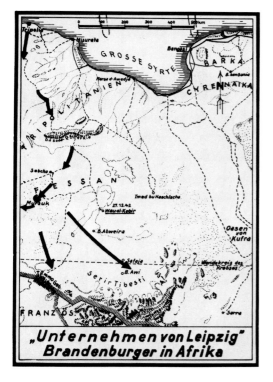

"Abt. von Koenen"

Captain von Koenen.

Commandos of the Brandenburgers in Adrica—opposing the Allied advance in the Tibesti Mountains . . .

. . . and in freight glider action near Gafsa in December of 1942.

Reorganization order by teletype on September 15, 1944—now the "Panzergrenadier Division Brandenburg."

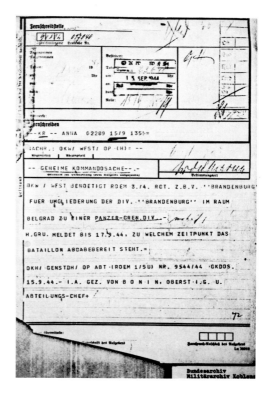

The Division Commander and his adjutant—Major General Schulte-Heuthaus and Captain Lau.

Soldiers of the Brandenburg Division (3rd
Battalion/1st Regiment BR) in action near
Skradin—September 1943.

Steel helmet and sleeve stripes—Signs of
membership in the "Panzerkorps
Grossdeutschland."

16.01.45 E-Transport über Thorn-Kutno
17.01.45 Entladen in Lentschütz, Russen bereits in der Nähe
18.01.45 Ortsverteidigung. Absetzen über Turek/Steinhofen
19.01.45 Kalisch
21.01.45 Steinhofen - Gartenau (3 km vor Kalisch). Ortsverteidigung.
22.01.45 Gartenau (Polko) - Kalisch. Ortsverteidigung.
23.01.45 Absetzen hinter Flutkanal, abends Kalisch aufgegeben
24.01.45 Sicherung in Langdorf. Maternhof. Oblt. Berger verwundet.
25.01.45 Maternhof-Baschau
25.01.45 Baschau-Koppelstädt
27.01.45 Koppelstädt - Kainzen bis Guhrau
28.01.45 Heidevorwerk bei Rüzen - Rüzen
31.01.45 Gutsvorwerk bei Rüzen - Rüzener Wald
01.02.45 Oder-Übergang - Altwasser
02.02.45 Altwasser - Hochkirch - Jauschwitz
03.02.45 Jauschwitz - Dammer
04.02.45 Dammer - Dornbuch - Heerwegen - Heimbach
08.02.45 Heimbach - Wuhleisen - Waltersdorf
09.02.45 Waltersdorf - Sprottau - Sagan - Mallmitz
10.02.45 Mallmitz - Sagan
11.02.45 Wöllersdorf - Sorau - Priebus
17.02.45 Priebus - Hermsdorf
19.02.45 Hermsdorf - Muskau
20.02.45 Döbern - Mühlrose
27.02.45 Mühlrose - Schleife - Weißwasser - Pechern - Neiße
05.03.45 Ablösung von der Neißestellung - Pechern - Schönlinden
06.03.45 Schönlinden - Neißestellung
25.03.45 Sägewerk bei Tränke
29.03.45 Sägewerk - Stellung bei Bergwerk
03.04.45 Bergwerk - Lodenau - Neißestellung
16.04.45 5.15 Uhr Beginn Trommelfeuer und russ. Großangriff
17.04.45 Absetzen nördlich Lodenau
18.04.45 Niederspree
19.04.45 Niederspree - Spähtrupp nach Daubitz
20.04.45 Niederspree - Eselsdorf - Angriff auf Klitten
21.04.45 Klitten - Angriff auf Tauern
22.04.45 Tauern - Angriff auf Förstgen
23.04.45 Förstgen
24.04.45 Angriff auf Weißenberg
25.04.45 Göda - Storchau
26.04.45 Storchau - Neulauske - Wetro
27.04.45 Wetro - Neschwitz. BtlKdr.Hptm. Hunold schwer verwundet,
          eine Stunde später ich selbst verwundet und damit für
          den Rest des Krieges abgemeldet.

Fighters and commandos in the East
and in Albania—in 1944.

Panzergrenadier—Division—Kurmark—the newest GD Division
Established in Cottbus early in February 1945.

Assault gun lying in wait.

Hand-drawn sketch map:
Podelzig battle zone—West of
the Oder from Klessin, in
March 1945.

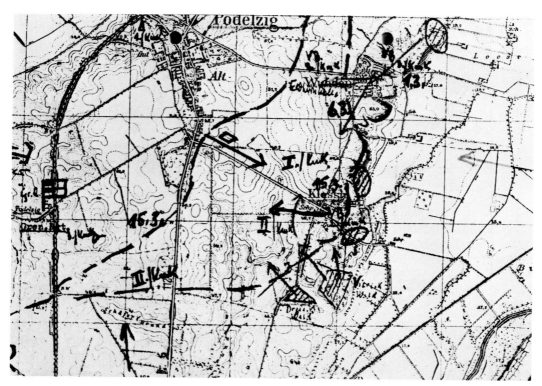

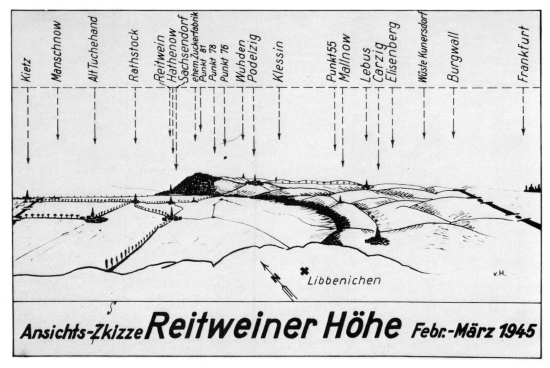

Kietz · Manschnow · Alt Tuchehand · Rathstock · Reitwein · Hathenow · Sachsendorf · ehem Zuckerfabrik · Punkt 81 · Punkt 78 · Punkt 76 · Wuhden · Podelzig · Klessin · Punkt 55 · Mallnow · Lebus · Cärzig · Elisenberg · Wüste Kunersdorf · Burgwall · Frankfurt

Libbenichen

v. H.

Ansichts-Zkizze **Reitweiner Höhe** Febr.-März 1945

Sketch map: Last German bastion before Berlin—the heights where the Germans suffered their heaviest losses.

Major von Courbiere, as of February 1945 Commander of the Panzergrenadier Regiment Kurmark.

German infantry, their morale broken!

174

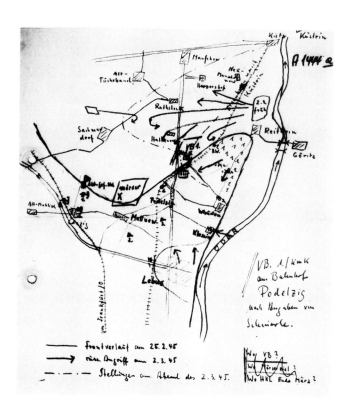

Hand-drawn sketch map: After the Soviet
breakthrough in the Reitwein Heights.

Only a few individual tanks are still in action.

Major General Langkeit
honors brave individual
fighting men with the
Knight's Cross—here:
Battalion Leader of the
2nd Battalion/Ensign
Regiment 1242—
subordinate to the
Kurmark—on March 25,
1945.

175

*—Securing before Halbe on April 28, 1945.

"Note": Out in the woods near Halbe, negatives found after the war are as follows*—six pictures: origin persumably Ic of the "January 30" Division. Thus poor quality.

*—Last troop assembly point near Forsthaus Hammer.

*—Hand-drawn sketch map: Breakthrough at Halbe on April 28 and 29, 1945.

*—"The line of escape northwest of Halbe, also called the Avenue of Death."

*—The "Avenue of Death" northwest of Halbe—Enemy fire from the front!!

*—Another attempted escape from the surrounded position in the forest west of Halbe on April 29, 1945.

Major Lehnhoff.

**The Last in Berlin—
Battle Group
Guard Regiment GD**

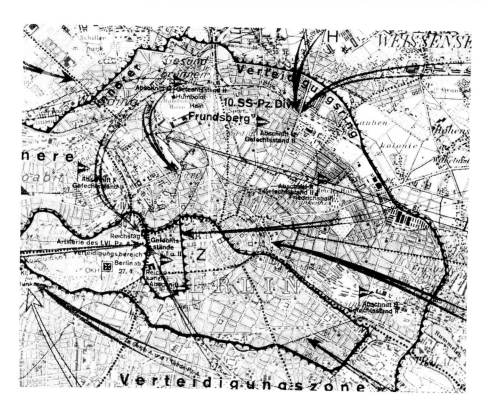

The national capital, Berlin, surrounded.

Major Lehnhoff and officers of the Guard Regiment GD—Berlin.

Soviet publication for the Berlin population, May 4, 1945.

≡ Nachrichtenblatt ≡

Nr. 2   Freitag, den 4. Mai 1945   Nr. 2

Nach der Einnahme von Berlin

In Berlin 134.000 Gefangene — Der Kessel südöstlich Berlin liquidiert — Dr. Fritsche berichtet über Selbstmord von Hitler und Goebbels — Vereinigung russischer und anglo-amerikanischer Truppen in Norddeutschland

Am 2. Mai gab das Informationsbüro der Sowjetunion bekannt:

Die Truppen der 1. Weißrussischen Front unter dem Oberbefehl von Marschall Shukow haben in Zusammenwirkung mit den Truppen der 1. Ukrainischen Front unter Marschall Konjew nach hartnäckigen Straßenkämpfen die deutsche Kräftegruppe in Berlin zerschlagen und heute, am 2. Mai, die Reichshauptstadt Berlin — das Zentrum des deutschen Imperialismus und den Herd der deutschen Eroberungspolitik — völlig in ihre Hand gebracht.

Die Besatzung von Berlin mit ihrem Kommandanten, General der Artillerie Weidling, an der Spitze stellte am 2. Mai um 15.00 Uhr den Widerstand ein und gab sich gefangen.

Am 2. Mai um 21.00 Uhr waren in Berlin bereits über 70.000 deutsche Soldaten und Offiziere in russische Gefangenschaft, darunter 8 Generale. U. a. wurde der erste Vertreter Goebbels' für Propaganda und Presse — Dr. phil. u. hist. Fritsche — gefangengenommen. Bei der Vernehmung sagte er aus, daß Hitler, Goebbels und der soeben ernannte Chef des Generalstabes, General der Infanterie Krebs, Selbstmord begangen hätten.

Die Wirtschaftsmacht des Sowjetstaates

Vor einigen Tagen wurde auf der 11. Tagung des Obersten Rates der UdSSR das Gesetz über das Staatsbudget der Sowjetunion für 1945 angenommen.

Das Budget der Sowjetunion im Jahre 1945 beträgt 307,7 Milliarden Rubel, d. i. fast 100 Milliarden Rubel mehr als im Vorjahre. 1944 sind die Staatseinnahmen der Sowjetunion um 58 Prozent gewachsen; für 1945 ist eine Steigerung von fast 40 Prozent vorgesehen.

Die militärischen Ausgaben für 1945 betragen 137,9 Milliarden Rubel, d. i. etwa 45 Prozent des Budgets. Neben den großen Ausgaben, die der Krieg zu seiner Vollendung erfordert, verfügt die Sowjetwirtschaft auch über genügend Mittel, einen großzügigen Kapitalaufbau durchzuführen, dessen Summe auf 46,8 Milliarden festgesetzt ist. Etwa die Hälfte davon wird für den Wiederaufbau der von den deutschen Eindringlingen zerstörten Wirtschaft in den befreiten Gebieten...

Field Guard Regiment GD under Lieutenant Colonel Hogrebe marching out of Berlin.

Graves of the Field Guard Regiment GD near Werneuchen—April 1945.

The Reichstag Building in Berlin
—May 1945.

The Chancellery in
Berlin—May 1945.

The last military report.

The Tannenberg
Memorial.

Interior of the Memorial, Berlin.

Holders of the Knight's Cross of the Iron Cross

(and the higher levels)—from all Grossdeutschland units. Awarded to them in those units and/or under other circumstances.

NAMES of those holders of the Knight's Cross GD on whom data are incomplete:

Technical Sgt. Franz Fischer,	2nd Pz. Regiment, Führer Escort Division.	Knight's Cross 4/30/1945
Sergeant Adolf Frankl,	Guard Regiment GD, Berlin,	Knight's Cross 4/26/1945
Captain Heinrich Klemt,	Pz. Engineer Battalion, Führer Grenadier Division,	Knight's Cross 5/2/1945
Sergeant ? Paul,	Guard Regiment GD, Berlin,	Knight's Cross at end of April 1945
Captain Otto Pfau, I.	(SPW)/Pz. Grenadier Regiment GD,	Knight's Cross 3/23/1945
Major Ruprecht Sommer,	Pz. Grenadier Regiment 4 Führer Grenadier Division,	Knight's Cross 4/5/1945

AFHELDT, Eckart, First Lieutenant
II./ Jäger Regiment 2 BR, Knight's Cross
3/17/1945
The Leader of the 2nd Battalion, Jäger Regiment
2 BR, First Lieutenant Afheldt . . . was able with
his weakened battalion, in a night attack on
January 31, 1945, to surprise the enemy and
penetrate into the town of Neu-Wiersewitz. With
that a threatened flank attack on the "Group von
Saucken" while crossing the Oder near Neu-
Fähreichen was eliminated.

ANDING, Friedrich, Lieutenant
Armored Jäger Unit GD, Knight's Cross
4/20/1945
In action against heavy British tanks in northern
Germany, Lieutenant Anding destroyed six
enemy tanks and five enemy armored reconnaissance cars by using a Panzerfaust as an
individual fighter on April 14/15, 1945 in
Stadensen and Nettelkamp.

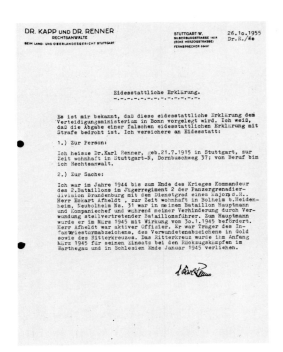

BASSE, Hans Dieter von, Major
1st/Pz. Fusilier Regiment GD, Knight's Cross
9/10/1944
Major von Basse earned the Knight's Cross on
August 16 when, in a bold individual attack, he
stormed the only still usable bridge in Kursenai
with a few men and occupied the enemy trench
system on the east shore.

BECK-BROICHSITTER, Helmut, First
Lieutenant
14th (Pz. Jäger) I.R. GD, Knight's Cross 9/4/1940
By holding off an enemy attack of the French 3rd
Armored Division near Stonne, destroying 83
enemy tanks from May 14 to 17, 1940, the 14th.
Panzer Jäger Company of the Infantry Regiment
GD, under the command of First Lieutenant
Beck-Broichsitter, made possible the completion
of the basin battle in Flanders.

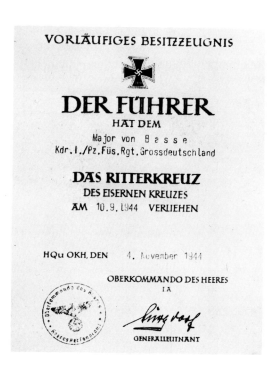

BERGMANN, Heinz, Master Sergeant
4th/Pz. Regiment 26 (GD), Knight's Cross
11/26/1944

After the capture of Wilkowischken, East Prussia, on August 10, 1944, Master Sergeant Bergmann was ordered to block a road occupied by some 25 enemy tanks. During the battle, he destroyed 19 enemy tanks and rolled over seven additional enemy antitank guns just put into position.

BIELIG, Martin, Master Sergeant
17th(s.IG)/Pz. Grenadier Regiment GD, Knight's
Cross 10/7/1944

Despite a severe hip wound in a Russian attack on September 18, 1944 in the Schaulen area, Master Sergeant Bielig made the decision to attack and repulse the Soviets with only five of his armored grenadiers. After that he reoccupied his B position and directed the s.IG fire against the enemy positions.

BLUMENTHAL, Carl-Ludwig, First Lieutenant
7th Company/I.R. GD, Knight's Cross 9/18/1942
On his own decision, and in a daring advance
with only five men of his company, First
Lieutenant Blumenthal stormed the Don bridge
at Woronesh on July 4, 1942. Thus he created the
conditions for the further attack against the city
and the formation of a bridgehead.

BOCK, Hans, Captain
III./Pz. Regiment GD, Knight's Cross 2/5/1945
Under the leadership of Captain Bock, a GD tank
unit advanced deep into the Russian encirclement
south of Königsberg early in February 1945 and
in this action destroyed 68 enemy tanks and 86
enemy antitank guns.

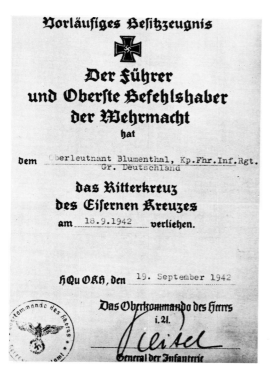

Vorläufiges Besitzeugnis

Der Führer
und Oberste Befehlshaber
der Wehrmacht
hat

dem Oberleutnant Blumenthal, Kp.Fhr.Inf.Rgt.
Gr. Deutschland

das Ritterkreuz
des Eisernen Kreuzes

am 18.9.1942 verliehen.

HQu OKH, den 19. September 1942

Das Oberkommando des Heeres
i.A.

General der Infanterie

Ritterkreuz für Panzerkommandeur

Der Führer verlieh das Ritterkreuz des Eisernen Kreuzes an
Hauptmann Hans Bock, Kom-
mandeur einer Panzerabteilung
unserer Division.

DF. Während der Kämpfe im ostpreußischen Raum zeichnete sich eine
gepanzerte Gruppe unter Führung von
Hauptmann Bock besonders aus. Im
Angriff stieß die Panzerkampfgruppe
bei G. tief in die Front der Sowjets
und sprengte nach weiteren erfolgreichen Einsätzen südlich Königsberg
die bolschewistische Umklammerung
der Stadt. Die Gruppe vernichtete während dieser Kämpfe insgesamt 68 Panzer und 86 Pak. In schwierigsten Lagen ermöglichten Angriffsgeist und
Tapferkeit des kühnen Panzerführers
diese hervorragenden Erfolge.

BOHNK, Georg, First Lieutenant
II./Pz. Fusilier Regiment GD, Knight's Cross
2/18/1945

In the Wormditt section of the front in East Prussia at the beginning of February 1945, First Lieutenant Böhnk and his battalion stopped an attempted enemy breakthrough. In heavy close combat, the city of Wormditt could be held.

BOHRENDT, Max, First Lieutenant
AA Platoon 52/I.D. GD, Knight's Cross 2/8/1943

During a reconnaissance advance near Tschebetovka at the end of January 1943, First Lieutenant Börendt recognized an enemy position at battalion strength. With his anti-aircraft platoon he moved around the Russian position and attacked it from the rear, smashed the enemy group and destroyed numerous trucks, grenade launchers and machine guns.

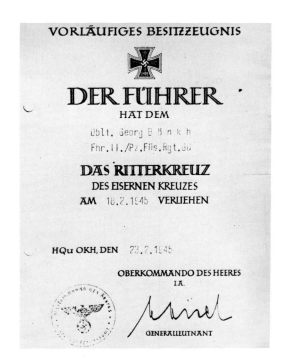

188

BROCKERHOFF, Wilhelm, Major
Pz. Artillery Regiment BR, Knight's Cross
5/8/1945
For outstanding leadership of the Panzer Artillery
Regiment Brandenburg and personal bravery in
the retreat actions before the Neisse in January
and February 1945, he was nominated to receive
the Knight's Cross, which was awarded to him at
the end of the war.

BRUCKNER, Erich von, Colonel
Commander, Jäger Regiment BR, Knight's Cross
3/11/1945
Colonel von Brückner, Commander of Jäger
Regiment 1 Brandenburg, was entrusted with
achieving the escape from Lissa. In the first days
of February 1945 he and the complement of the
fortress reached the city of Glogau without
serious losses.

DÖNITZ

z. Zt. Rom, 18.4.6...

Bescheinigung.

Ich bescheinige, daß ich dem
Major a.D. Wilhelm
Bröckerhoff am 8.5.45
das Ritterkreuz ver-
liehen habe.

Dönitz

Großadmiral a. D.

HERMANN PFROMMER   75 PFORZHEIM, 9. 4. 81

Lieber Erich !

Zu Deinem Anruf wegen der Verdienste, die zur Verleihung des
Ritterkreuzes an unseren früheren Rgt.Kdr. Oberst v. Brückner
führten, kann ich Dir aus meiner Erinnerung folgendes sagen:

Um die Jahreswende 1944/45 wurde ich als Ia-Schreiber vom I.Btl.
zum Rgt.-Stab versetzt. Ich kam Anfang Januar 1945 in Angerburg an.
Schon wenige Tage nach meiner Ankunft wurden wir verladen und sollten
angeblich in den Raum Litzmannstadt (Lodz) verlegt werden. Unterwegs
wurden wir von der russischen Offensive überrascht und ziemlich
zerstreut. Unser Rgt.Stab und einige Teile unseres Rgt. kamen nach
Lissa.

Lissa war inzwischen zur Festung erklärt. Wir saßen fest. Festungs-
Kommandant war ein General Henrici oder Heinrici . Dieser hielt sich
praktisch nur in unserem Rgt.Gef.Stand bei Oberst v. Brückner auf.

Da ich selbst erst ganz kurz beim Rgt.Stab war, kann ich heute nicht
mehr genau sagen, welche Offiziere unserer Division in Lissa waren.
Gisbert Scholte kannte, ob ich schon an der 17.Kp. kannte, war dabei.Ob
Oblt.Grosser, der bei Kriegsende Rgt.Adjutant war, da war, weiß ich
nicht mehr.

Die Lage in diesen Tagen war jedenfalls so, daß wir in Lissa saßen,
der Russe aber rechts und links an uns vorbei war. Wir waren zur
Untätigkeit verurteilt. An einem Nachmittag sollte ein Sanka Verwundete ausfahren, vermutlich in Richtung Glogau. Unter den Verwundeten befand sich Lt. Vietor. Der Sanka kam nie am Ziel an.

In einer Unterhaltung mit Oblt. Schulte und weiteren Offz. erlaubte
ich mir, ihnen nahe zu legen, sie möchten doch versuchen Oberst
von Brückner dafür zu gewinnen, daß den Festungs-Kommandanten zu
überzeugen versuche, daß ein Verbleiben der in Lissa befindlichen
deutschen Truppen -man sprach von etwa 2000 Mann- nutzlos geworden
sei. Es konnten ja keine feindlichen Truppen mehr gebunden werden,
was doch Sinn der "Festungen" war.

Plötzlich ging alles schnell, sodaß ich selbst nicht mehr alle
Einzelheiten der Befehle mitbekam.

Am Abend wurde der Abzug der deutschen Truppen befohlen (wohl vom
Festungs-Kommandanten). Oberst von Brückner dürfte mit der Durchführung des Ausbruchs beauftragt gewesen sein. In aller Eile wurde
eine Kampfgruppe zusammengestellt, die den Ausbruch sicherte.
Am nächsten Morgen waren wir -ohne Verluste- in Glogau.

Von dort wurden wir sofort in den Oder-Brückenkopf von Steinau geworfen.

Oberst von Brückner kam dann vom Rgt. weg; soll aber für den Ausbruch -vermutlich auf Vorschlag des Festungs-Kommandanten- das
Ritterkreuz erhalten haben.

BURG, Jörg, First Lieutenant
7th/Pz. Regiment GD, Oak leaves (604.) to
Knight's Cross 10/4/1944
On August 19, 1944 First Lieutenant Burg and
his tanks broke through an enemy antitank
position in rough country in the Schaulen area,
destroyed six enemy antitank guns there and
repulsed a Russian counterattack against the
German flank.

CZORNY, Wilhelm, Corporal
2nd Company/Pz. Grenadier Regiment GD,
Knight's Cross 10/4/1944
During an advancing action before Doblen at the
end of September 1944, Corporal Czorny was able
to put two enemy antitank guns of a line out of
action and thus contribute significantly to the
success of the whole attack.

DIDDENS, Diddo, First Lieutenant
1st/Assault Brigade GD, Oak leaves to the
Knight's Cross 6/15/1944
On April 25, 1944 First Lieutenant Diddens,
fighting against highlands heavily occupied with
antitank guns on the east bank of the Sereth,
acted on his own initiative and penetrated far
into the enemy rear, destroyed three tanks and 31
enemy antitank guns, and returned to the main
battle line.

FABICH, Maxemilian, Lieutenant Colonel
Pz. Fusilier Regiment GD, Knight's Cross,
5/8/1945
In severe close combat near Vw. Korschelken on
March 4 and 5, 1945 the enemy was driven out of
the advance position through the steadfastness
and action of Lieutenant Colonel Fabich, a
threatened flank attack was made impossible,
and considerable enemy materiel destroyed.

191

FAMULA, Günther, Lieutenant
5th (Pz.) Fusilier Escort Battalion, Knight's Cross
5/4/1944

During fighting in the swampy area of the Narwa bridgehead on April 19, 1944, Lieutenant Famula led the foremost tanks of the Strachwitz battle group with bravery and coolness. In a further advance, Famula was severely wounded in a thickly wooded area and succumbed on April 22, 1944.

FOELKERSAM, Adrian von, Lieutenant
Training Regiment BR zbV 800, Knight's Cross
9/14/1942

Lieutenant von Foelkersam was in a camouflaged position at the head of German troops north of Maikop in July of 1942. He had the task of protecting petroleum pipelines in the area from destruction. In the NKWD center of Maikop he prevented the advance of Russian reserves and made it possible for German troops to penetrate into Maikop on August 9, 1942.

FRANCOIS, Edmund, Captain
Pz. Grenadier Brigade von Werthern, Knight's Cross 10/20/1944

In August and September of 1944, Captain Francois commanded an anti-aircraft battery in the Panzer Grenadier Brigade von Werthern and stood out through personal courage and outstanding leadership of the battle group in Lithuania. He fell in East Prussia on March 6, 1945.

FRANTZ, Peter, Captain
Assault Unit GD, Knight's Cross 6/4/1942, Oak leaves (228.) 4/14/1943

First Lieutenant Frantz achieved a great defensive victory in the Tula area on December 13, 1941. With his assault guns he destroyed 15 enemy tanks. This increased the total number of Russian tanks destroyed by the 16th (Assault) Company, commanded by him, to 46. In tank battles on March 14, 1943 east of Borisovka, Assault Unit DG, under the command of Captain Frantz, was able to destroy 43 enemy T-34 tanks. For this resounding success he was decorated with the oak leaves to the Knight's Cross.

Hauptmann Edmund Francois
Battr.Chef"Fla.Flak-Battr. FBB
Ritterkreuz: 20.Oktober 1944
gefallen: 6.März 45 /Ostpreussen

K'Grp.Kdr."Pz.Gr.Brig.v.Werthern
August/Sept. 1944

Hauptmann Francois war in jeder Hinsicht vorbildlicher Offizier. Ihn zeichneten Verantwortungsfreude und Entschlusskraft besonders aus. Er war ein sehr tapferer Soldat, der sich ohne Rücksicht auf die eigene Person voll einsetzte, dabei dennoch stets bemüht war, das Leben der ihm anvertrauten Soldaten möglichst zu schonen. Stets wohlüberlegt handelnd, zeigte er überdurchschnittliche Leistungen.

Für seine persönliche Tapferkeit, klare Befehlserteilung und hervorragende Führung der Kampfgruppe wurde er am 20.10.1944 mit dem Ritterkreuz ausgezeichnet. Er fiel am 6.März 1945 in Ostpreussen.

Oberstleutnant a.B. und ehem.Kdr.
der Pz.Gren.Brigade " von Werthern "

Für alle Teile des Regiments die Upa am 11. Dez. 1941 mit ihren bewaldeten Höhen auf dem Westufer. Der Flußübergang auf einer Kriegsbrücke bei Truschkina und Kamenka.

Und dann Jassnaja Poljana am 12. Dez. 41, wo sich der Rgt.Gef.Std. erneut einrichtet. Dort, wo das Grab Leo Tolstois im nahen Walde zu finden ist, wo vor Wochen schon einmal das Regiment war, noch im Angriff nach Norden, nach Tula. In diesem Zeitpunkt ist die Führung des Regiments um einen geordneten Rückzug besorgt, sucht sie die Zügel fest in der Hand zu halten. Aber die schneller als angenommen vordringenden Russen vor und zwischen den Bataillonen zwingen zu Einzelaktionen; die höheren Kommandobehörden unterstellen entgegen dem Wunsch der Rgt.-Führung einzelne Einheiten anderen, fremden Divisionen.

Das II. Bataillon, mit Unterstützung der Art.Abt. 400 bei Kishkino, sieht sich in heftigen Abwehrkämpfen auf dem Westufer der Upa, wo sich noch am 13. Dezember 41 bei der Ortschaft Upakaja Fati schwere Gefechte abspielen. – Das I. Btl., inzwischen einer fremden Division unterstellt, steht ebenfalls in heftigen Gefechten südwestl. von Tula. Und dabei Sturmgeschütze der 16.Stu.Gesch.Kp. unter Oblt. Frantz, der am 13. Dezember einen großen Abwehrerfolg erringt: Mit seinem Zuge kann er in wenigen Stunden 15 feindliche Panzer vernichten und damit die Abschuß-Erfolge der 16.Stu.Gesch.Kp. im bisherigen Verlauf des Rußlandkrieges auf insgesamt 46 erhöhen. – Der jetzt angreifende Gegner führt mit seinen frischen Kräften eine große Anzahl Panzer mit sich, um den Durchbruch in jedem Fall zu erzwingen.

Etwa um die gleiche Zeit, als der großartige Erfolg des Zuges Oblt. Frantz auf dem Rgt.Gef.Std. in Kolpna Nowaja am 14. Dezember bekannt wird, kann die 14.Pz.Jäg.Kp. im gleichen Kampfraum, und auch beim I. Bataillon ihren 100. Panzerabschuß melden. Darüber und zugleich über den Erfolg der Sturmgeschütze berichtet ein Angehöriger der 1. Kp. des I. Btl., wobei deutlich wird, wie sich der opfervolle, tapfere Einsatz des einzelnen Grenadiers über die Mechanik des Panzer-Kampfes erhebt.

GARSKI, Eugen, Lieutenant Colonel
III./I.R. GD, Knight's Cross 7/19/1940
On May 10, 1940, Lieutenant Colonel Garski led the air-land operation NIWI and defended himself deep in enemy country with only nine of his men. After reinforcements arrived, he occupied the towns of Traimont and Witry and thus made the march to Belgium possible.

GEHRKE, Kurt, Lieutenant Colonel
I./Grenadier Regiment GD, Knight's Cross
2/8/1943
On December 3, 1942 strong Russian attacks began, particularly before Kusovlevo in the central sector. Lieutenant Gehrke and his battalion were able to hold out bravely in a bad situation and destroy 13 of 14 attacking enemy tanks using antitank and close combat weapons.

Auf dem Verlegungsmarsch ist mit Feind auf der Rollbahn zu rechnen, eine Annahme, die sich dann freilich als falsch herausstellt. Es wird also ernst mit der seit Tagen beantragten Verstärkung. Die erste Erleichterung bei den Kampfgruppen der I.D. GD im Lutschessa-Tal macht sich bemerkbar: Das Kradschtz.Btl. GD ist im Anmarsch, Pioniere und abgestellte Panzer der Pz.Abt. GD sind im Anrollen; auch das bei der 206. I.D. noch immer eingesetzte III. Btl./Gren.Rgt. hat Befehl, nach Ablösung in den Kampfraum seiner Division zu verlegen. — Auch die II. Abt./A.R. GD bereitet sich auf die Verlegung ihrer Batterien in das Lutschessa-Tal vor. Die Männer können ein wenig aufatmen. Es ist aber auch höchste Zeit!

Bei der Kampfgruppe Lindemann im Nordwestteil des Kampfabschnitts gehen die Kämpfe mit unverminderter Heftigkeit weiter. Auch am 3. Dezember greift der Gegner ununterbrochen mit starken Kräften an. So gelingt es ihm, zahlreiche Einbrüche zu erzielen und damit zunächst eine völlig offene und ungeklärte Lage zu schaffen. Der Feinddruck hat sich dort um die Mittagszeit vor allem durch zahlreiche Panzer so erheblich verstärkt, daß der linke Flügel der Kampfgruppe Lindemann zurückgenommen werden muß. Die bisherigen Besatzungen in Niwje und Griwa schlagen sich auf eine neue Linie Kornilowka – Mal. Iwanowka – Punkt 249,1 durch, wo sie mit ihrem linken Flügel wieder Anschluß an das in Pysino und Lonow stehende II. Btl./Gren. Rgt. GD gewinnen. Rege feindliche Fliegertätigkeit mit Bomben- und Tieffliegerangriffen herrscht im gesamten Raum. Auch bei der Kampfgruppe Lorenz (Pioniere und I./Grenadiere) setzen bereits gegen 7.00 Uhr früh erste feindliche Angriffe mit Panzerunterstützung ein, die nach heftigen Kämpfen einen Einbruch in den Ort Wereista erzielen. Bei den Gefechten, die sich vor Kusowlewo entwickeln – Feindpanzer gegen Grenadiere der I. Btl. – gelingt es bis zum Abend, von 14 Angreifern insgesamt 13 zu vernichten – mit Panzerabwehr, Nahkampfmitteln und den wenigen Sturmgeschützen, die da sind. Hierbei fallen u. a. der Uffz. Hermann Nagel und Gefr. Joh. Bösing der Stu.Gesch.Abt. GD, nachdem sie noch mehrere Feind-Panzer haben abschießen können.

Der Kommandeur des I./Gren., Obstlt. (seit 1. 4. 1942) Gehrke wird für sein tapferes Aushalten in und bei Kusowlewo zum Ritterkreuz eingereicht, nachdem er immer wieder einen Durchbruch an dieser Stelle mit seinen Männern verhindern konnte.

GEISBERG, Wilhelm, First Lieutenant
3rd/Pz. Regiment FBD, Knight's Cross 4/14/1945
In the Jägerndorf/Paulinenhof area First Lieutenant Geisberg moved into an enemy assembly of tanks on March 28 and 29, 1945 and by making clever use of the landscape was able to destroy some 25 tanks. Geisberg himself destroyed six of the enemy tanks.

GRABERT, Siegfried, Captain
Training Regiment BR zbV 800, Knight's Cross
6/10/1941, Oak leaves 11/6/1943
On April 12, 1941 Lieutenant Grabert and his men were able, in zbV action, to capture the Vardar bridge at Axioupolis, imoportant for further advance, in a bold move. Captain Grabert and his 8th Company captured the six strongly defended Don bridges south of Rostov near Bataisk on July 25, 1942. Grabert himself and sixteen of his men died heroically there.

Gefecht bei Paulinenhof
Fasanerie- Hennerwitz
28./ 29.März 1945

Oberleutnant Wilhelm Geisberg
Kp.Chef 3./Pz.Rgt.
Ritterkreuz: 14.April 1945

Es war am 28.3. oder 29.3.1945 , jedenfalls die letzten März-Tage im Raum JÄGERNDORF - TROPPAU (Sudet.-Land)- bei Paulinen-hof - Hennerwitz . Durch Aufklärung wurde in unserem Abschnitt der 5.(Pz.)Kp. (?) - eine feindl. Panzeransammlung von über 30 Fd.-Panzer gemeldet.
Oblt. G e i s b e r g entschloss sich - um nicht überrollt zu werden, mit seinen noch verfügbaren (ich glaube , wir waren noch 11 Panzer einsatzfähig ..) Panzern sofort anzugreifen.
Durch seine geschickte Führung , unter Ausnutzung des Geländes und durch Einteilung in mehrere Gruppen gelang die Überraschung den "egner bis auf drei oder 4 Fd.-Panzer völlig zu vernichten.
Bei den eigenen Panzern war nur Blech-Schaden - wie man zu sa-gen pflegte.
G e i s b e r g schoss dabei selbst - so glaube ich zu wissen, mindestens 6 Fd.-Panzer ab.
Diese gelungene Tat brachte ihm bei der Kompanie den Spitz-namen: T - 3 4 Willi " - ein..
In der Kompanie brachte es reichlich EK.II und EK.I ein, sogar einige Deutsche Kreuz in Gold gab es..

GREIM, Alfred, Lieutenant Colonel
II./I.R. GD 1, Knight's Cross 6/4/1942
The II./I.R. GD under the command of
Lieutenant Colonel Greim, in severe defensive
fighting in the Kishkino/Tula area on December
13, 1941 and were able to hold their position
stubbornly against heavy enemy attacks.

HANERT, Karl, First Lieutenant
4th/I.R. GD, Knight's Cross 8/23/1941
In the days from July 21 to 26, 1941 First
Lieutenant Hänert—fighting in the foremost
line—held off strong enemy flank threats near
Jelnja. Often it was only in severe hand-to-hand
combat that the enemy could be driven back. Karl
Hänert fell at Kruglovka/Jelnja on October 14.

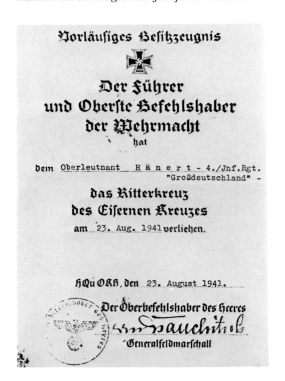

HEESEMANN, Wolfgang, Colonel
Commander, Pz. Grenadier Regiment GD,
Knight's Cross 2/17/1945

HEINRICH, Willi, First Lieutenant
1st/Tank Unit FGB, Knight's Cross 12/9/1944
In the action south of Gross Waltersdorf, an
enemy tank group advanced toward Gumbinnen
as of October 20, 1944. In a lightning counterattack, Lieutenant Heinrich attacked the head of
the Soviet tanks near Gross Tellerode and was
able to scatter them.

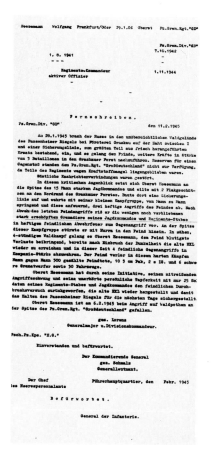

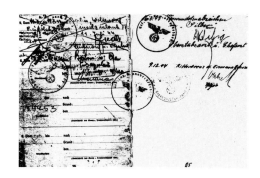

HENSEL, Herbert, Captain
Pz. Fusilier Battalion/FGD, Knight's Cross
3/5/1945

The hard battles in the Ardennes offensive in December 1944 and January 1945 were handled by the Panzer Fusiliers of the Führer Grenadier Brigade under Captain Hensel just as well as later in the Arnswalde and Lauban areas in February 1945. Captain Hensel was always with his hard-fighting men and was able to attain decisive victories with them.

HERBST, Josef, First Lieutenant
II./Fusilier Regiment GD, Knight's Cross
9/30/1943

With his battalion, First Lieutenant Herbst had to withstand hard times near Kotelva in mid-August 1943, when strong enemy forces attacked several times a day. Despite the loss of a leg, Herbst was always at the head of his men in close combat and led them to success through his example.

HINDELANG, Hans, Master Sergeant
14th (Pz. Jäger)/I.R. GD, Knight's Cross 9/4/1940
At Stonne in France on May 15, 1940, Master
Sergeant Hindelang and his antitank platoon
held off a heavy tank attack to the flank of the
attacking regiment and destroyed 57 tanks.

HOERNLEIN, Walter, Lieutenant General
Infantry Division (motorized) GD, Oak leaves
(213.) to Knight's Cross 3/15/1943
Under the leadership of General Hoernlein, the
Infantry Division (motorized) GD, in the time
from March 7 to 23, 1943, attained the greatest
offensive success as they advanced from the
Kharkov area in the direction of Borrisovka—
Graiworon and smashed a Russian armored
corps. For the alert leadership of his division, W.
Hoernlein was decorated with the oak leaves
(213.) to the Knight's Cross.

Vorläufiges Besitzzeugnis

Der Führer
und Oberste Befehlshaber
der Wehrmacht

hat

dem   Oberfeldw. Hindelang
       J.R.Groß-Deutschland

das Ritterkreuz
des Eisernen Kreuzes

am   4.Sept. 1940 verliehen.

H.Qu.OKH, den 9.September 1940
Der Oberbefehlshaber des Heeres

Brauchitsch
Generalfeldmarschall

VORLÄUFIGES BESITZZEUGNIS

DER FÜHRER
HAT DEM

Generalleutnant Hoernlein,
Kommandeur Pz.Gr.Div."Großdeutschland"

DAS EICHENLAUB
ZUM RITTERKREUZ DES EISERNEN KREUZES
AM 15.3.1943   VERLIEHEN

HQu OKH, DEN   14.Oktober 1944.

OBERKOMMANDO DES HEERES
I.A.

Siegroth
Generalleutnant

HOLM, Max, Master sergeant
II./Pz. Regiment FBB, Knight's Cross 1/19/1945
In the Ardennes offensive on January 17, 1945,
Master Sergeant Holm stood out by coolly
moving into the tank battle at Chifontaine with
his assault gun and destroying seven American
tanks himself.

HUCKEL, Ernst-Albrecht, Captain
Pz. Engineer Battalion GD, Knight's Cross
9/27/1943
Through the decision of Captain Hückel, assault
engineers penetrated the village of Staraja-
Rjabina on August 9, 1943, wiped out numerous
nests of opposition in hand-to-hand combat, and
drove the enemy out of the town.

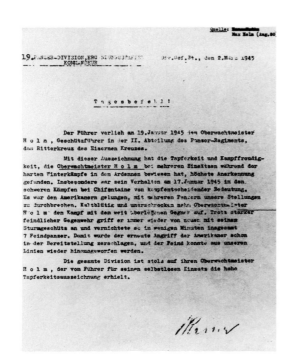

KAHSNITZ, Erich, Colonel
Pz. Fusilier Regiment GD, Knight's Cross
7/15/1943
At the head of his fusiliers, Colonel Kahsnitz broke through the Russian field positions near Gerzovka on July 5, 1943, took the heights and occupied them. In this attack Colonel Kahsnitz was fatally wounded.

KAPSREITER, Franz, Master Sergeant
4th/Assault Brigade FGB, Knight's Cross
1/14/1945
Within the Führer Grenadier Brigade, Master Sergeant Kapsreiter fought during the Ardennes offensive and showed himself to be a steadfast and courageous leader of his assault platoon.

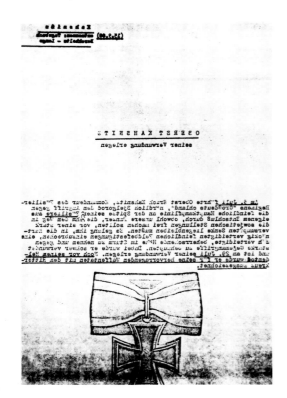

KESSEL, Willi, Master Sergeant
3rd/Pz. A.A. GD, Knight's Cross 2/23/1944
Through energetic action with only a few of his
men, Master Sergeant Kessel attacked the enemy
position near Szokolovo on the Dniepr on
October 5, 1943 and occupied a commanding
height. Despite suffering wounds, he held the
heights against repeated enemy attacks.

KIRSTEN, Rudi, Captain
Pz. Grenadier e.u.A.Unit GD, Guben, Knight's
Cross 3/28/1945
In the fighting around Guben at the end of
February 1945, Captain Kirsten, on his own
initiative, led a counteraction in the sectors
threatened by the Russians. With his troops he
was able to hold the contested positions until
reinforcements arrived.

VORLÄUFIGES BESITZZEUGNIS

DER FÜHRER
HAT DEM

Oberwachtmeister K e s s e l ,
Zugführer 3./Pz.Aufkl.Abt."Grossdeutschland"

DAS RITTERKREUZ
DES EISERNEN KREUZES
AM 23.2.1944 VERLIEHEN

HQu OKH, DEN 24.Februar 1944

OBERKOMMANDO DES HEERES
I.A.

GENERALLEUTNANT

KLEMM, Hans, Sergeant
2nd/I.R. GG 1, Knight's Cross 12/10/1942
After all officers and junior leaders had fallen,
Sergeant Klemm took command of two companies on September 30, 1942 and penetrated
enemy positions south of Belogurovo. There he
defended himself stubbornly until reinforcements
arrived.

KLEMZ, Bernhard, Captain
5th/Pz. Regiment GD, Knight's Cross 6/4/1944
During the heavy fighting north of Targul
Frumos on April 27, 1944, Captain Klemz made
the independent decision to attack a waiting
enemy unit with his 19 Panzer IV tanks and wipe
it out. In the process he destroyed 20 enemy tanks,
some 13 enemy antitank guns, artillery pieces
and trucks, without losing any of his unit.

Dennoch sind die Angriffserfolge erheblich. Für den Uffz. Klemm von
der 2. Kp./I.R. GD 1 ist der 30. September 1942 zugleich der Glückstag.
Nach Ausfall des Kp.-Chefs und aller Feldwebel übernimmt er die
Führung der 2. Kompanie und erreicht unter vollem Einsatz seiner
Person nicht nur das befohlene Angriffsziel, sondern trägt den Angriff
durch selbst gefaßten Entschluß weit darüber hinaus. Für seine vorbildliche Tat verleiht ihm der Oberste Befehlshaber das Ritterkreuz
zum Eisernen Kreuz.

Die Begründung für die Verleihung wird vom Regiment so gefaßt:
„Am 30. September 1942 befand sich die 2. Kompanie am linken
Flügel des I. Btl./I.R. 1 GROSSDEUTSCHLAND im Angriff auf die

vom Feind zäh verteidigten Mulden des Gostischka-Bachgrundes
südostwärts Tschermassowo.
Im stärksten feindlichen Gewehrfeuer fielen der Kompanie-Chef und
dessen Stellvertreter wenige Minuten nach Angriffsbeginn.
Als auch bei der rechten Nachbarkompanie der Kompanieführer und
dessen Vertreter fast gleichzeitig ausgefallen waren, drohte der
Angriff der beiden nun führerlos gewordenen Kompanien vor dem
Erreichen des Angriffszieles liegenzubleiben. –
In dieser äußerst schwierigen Lage trat der Feind aus Boltino heraus
von 2 Panzern unterstützt zum Gegenstoß an, um das I. Bataillon
auf seine Ausgangsstellungen zurückzuwerfen.
Da übernahm Uffz. Klemm entschlossen die Führung beider Kompanien, riß sie zum Angriff vor und brachte sie an das befohlene Angriffsziel. Hier erkannte er, daß das rechte Nachbarregiment (I.R. 2), das
an dem I. Bataillon vorbei auf Boltino vorstoßen sollte, nicht vorwärts
kam. Sofort faßte er den selbständigen Entschluß, mit den schwachen,
ihm verbliebenen Teilen hinter dem abgeschlagenen Gegenstoß der
Russen über die stark ausgebauten feindl. Stellungen nachstoßend
das Höhengelände südlich Belogurowo, 500 m westl. Boltino, zu
nehmen und sich dort zur Verteidigung einzurichten.
Dieser kühne Entschluß war die Voraussetzung, daß das für die
Division befohlene Angriffsziel trotz des Zurückbleibens des rechten
Nachbarregimentes (I.R. 2), frühzeitig erreicht wurde.
Diese Tat, die die persönliche Tapferkeit und Entschlußkraft des
Uffz. Klemm in schwieriger Lage besonders herausstellte, hat der
Division den erstrebten Erfolg gebracht." –
Die I.D. GD hat allein am 30. September 1942 folgende Erfolge zu
verzeichnen: 288 Gefangene, 525 Feindtote, Vernichtung oder Er-
beutung von 1 IG., 8 s.MG., 27 l.MG., 19 Pak, 19 Granatwerfern,
5 Pz.-Büchsen, 389 Karabinern, 21 MPi., 14 Panzern und 7 Art.-Ge-
schützen; dieser Tag bringt der Division die volle Anerkennung des
Oberbefehlshabers der 9. Armee (Gen.Obst. Model). –

KNAAK, Hans-Wolfram, First Lieutenant
8th/Training Regiment BR zbV 800, Knight's
Cross 11/3/1942

The target of the zbV action on June 26, 1941 was
the highway bridge at Dünaburg. which was
decisive for the further advance of the 8th Panzer
Division. Ahead of the German front line, First
Lieutenant Knaak and his command stormed the
bridge and defended themselves in desperate
fighting and at the cost of his life, until German
troops arrived.

KOENEN, Friedrich von, Captain
4th Regiment Division BR, Knight's Cross
9/16/1943

Captain von Koenen undertook an air-land
operation from Bizerta, North Africa, on
December 26, 1942, against a railroad bridge over
the Wadi el Kbir. The bridge was finally blown
up, breaking an important supply line of the
Allies.

Oberleutnant Hans-Wolfram K n a a k - 8./Baulehr-Regiment zbV 800

Während die 1.Panzer-Division als Stosskeil des XXXXI.Pz.-Korps am
24.Juni 1 9 4 1 gegen Mittag aufgehalten wird und in einer Kehrtwendung
nach Südwesten - den von Osten in die rechte Flanke zielenden Pz.-An-
griff des sowjet. III.Pz.-Korps abwehren muss, kann die 8.Panzer-Division
unter General Brandenberger als Spitze des LVI.Pz.-Korps entlang der
Strasse WILKOMIERZ - UTENA - auf DÜNABURG vorstossen. Aus ihm heraus star
tet ein Kommando der BRANDENBURGER unter Führung des Oblt. K n a a k mit
Ziel " Düna"-Brücken vor der Stadt.
Major Gebhard der 8.Pz.-Division - dabei als V.O. der Lt. Horst Glänzel
vom Baulehr-Rgt.zbV 800 - berichtet:

" Nach Überschreiten der ostpreussisch - litauischen Grenze ist es für
den weiteren Vormarsch der 8.Pz.Div. von entscheidender Bedeutung, die
grosse Strassenbrücke über die " Düna " unversehrt in die Hand zu be-
kommen.

Während des nächtlichen Vormarsches schiebt sich in die Vorhut - noch
vor meinen Wagen - ein Pkw ein. Wie ich feststelle, handelt es sich
um das Zugführer'fahrzeug eines uns zugeteilten Zuges des " Regiments
zbV 800 ".-

Über Auftrag und Zweck der Zuteilung schweigt sich der mir unbekannte
Oberleutnant aus. Wir wissen von diesem Regiment nur, dass es dem OKW
unmittelbar untersteht, für besondere Aufgaben eingeteilt und mit dem
Nimbus des Geheimnisses umwittert ist.

Im Morgengrauen des 26.Juni 1941 fährt dann der Zug der "BRANDENBURGER'
auf zwei sowjetischen Beute -Lkw , noch der eigenen Vorhut voraus,
nach Osten .- Dem einen Lastwagen gelingt es , unbehelligt über die
"Düna"-Brücke zu kommen. Erst an der anderen Brückenauffahrt wird er
erkannt und beschossen ; jedoch kann sich seine Besatzung vom Lkw lö-
sen und Stellung beziehen.

Der andere Beute- Lkw wird jedoch bereits auf der Strassenbrücke durch
sowjet. s.MG. erfasst und die Besatzung zum vorzeitigen Absitzen gezwungen. Nur unter Verlusten kann sie den Anschluss nach drüben erreichen.

Es gelingt den BRANDENBURGERN dieses Zuges trotz schweren feindl. Feuers, die Stellungen jenseits der Brücke zu behaupten und den Übergang
bis zum Eintreffen der Panzerspitze offen zu halten.

Die Masse der Angehörigen des Zuges ist gefallen ; dabei auch der Ober
leutnant und Führer dieses Unternehmens.

Die Überlebenden sind fast ausnahmslos verwundet. Die Gefallenen finden ihre letzte Ruhestätteauf dem rechten Flussp-Ufer unmittelbar am
Brücken-Ausgang.

Bei diesem Unternehmen fielen u.a.:   entnommen:Buch-R.Stoves

Oblt. Hs.-W. K n a a k
Gefr. Heinz Rösler   Gefr. Anton Stauder
Gefr. Karl Innerhofer   Oschtz. Mathias Plattner

KOHLHAAS, Ludwig, Lieutenant Colonel
III./I.R. GD 2, Knight's Cross 11/21/1942
In fast action on June 28, 1942, the bridge over
the Tim was taken by the 3rd Battalion of I.R.
GD 2 under the command of Lieutenant Colonel
Kohlhaas. This was of decisive importance for
the further advance of the division. Lieutenant
Colonel Kohlhaas was severely wounded in the
process by a mistaken bomb attack of German
aircraft.

KONOPKA, Gerhard, First Lieutenant
II./Grenadier Regiment GD, Knight's Cross
8/29/1943
On August 3, 1943 the 2nd Battalion of the GD,
under the command of First Lieutenant
Konopka, attacked the "Yellow Heights" near
Alissova and, despite vigorous opposition, was
able to achieve its objective. In the process, the
battalion formed a new line of battle with the best
view far into enemy country.

28. Juni 1942

Hinter ihnen, besonders am Bahndamm, quälen sich zunächst die
Sturmgeschütze ab, irgendeine Auffahrt auf den Dammaufwurf zu
finden, um die Brücke der Eisenbahn als Übergang über den Fluß
zu benutzen. Verstärkung für die 11. Kp., die vorn ohne schwere Waffen
liegt, ist dringend erforderlich. Es gelingt zunächst nicht; als ein vor-
witziger Panzer der Pz.Abt. GD schließlich doch auf dem Bahndamm
die Brücke erreicht, bleibt er hängen, stellt sich quer und liegt fest.
Nun ist alles versperrt; die anderen Panzer stehen in Reihe dahinter und
können weder vor noch zurück. Und während die Schützen der anderen
Kompanien sich daran machen, den Fluß zu Fuß nach Osten zu überschreiten, erlebt die verstärkte 11. Kp. ein Drama, das noch Tage
später bedrückend nachhängt. Hierüber berichtet Lt. Kersting als Zugführer des IG.-Zuges der 15. Kp., der als Verstärkung bei der 11. Kp.
den erfolgreichen Vorstoß begleitet hat:

„Wir stoßen nach dem Übergang über den Tim etwa 2000 Meter
weiter nach Osten vor bis zu einem Höhenrücken bei Swoboda-
Poshidajewka. Dort hatten die Russen Gräben ausgeworfen, die wir
gleich besetzen, denn jeden Augenblick ist mit einem feindlichen
Gegenstoß zu rechnen. Weiter links sammeln währenddessen die
Russen in einer vorwärts gelegenen Mulde. –

Ich war gerade dabei, die Geschütze in Stellung zu bringen und die
B.-Stellen einzurichten, als neun Horizontal- und Sturzkampfbomber
anflogen. Wir haben sofort unsere orange-farbenen Fliegertücher
sowie Hakenkreuz-Fahnen ausgebreitet und Rauchzeichen abge-
brannt. Und doch wurden wir derart mit Bomben belegt, daß der
IG.-Zug (l.IG.) nach dem Abziehen der Rauch- und Staubwolken
bei erster Übersicht noch eine Stärke von 1 Offizier, einem Unteroffizier und 8 Mann hatte. Ferner war noch ein Geschütz einsatz-
bereit, ein Kübelwagen sowie ein beschädigtes Krad; alles andere war
draufgegangen. Die menschlichen Ausfälle waren noch gar nicht zu
übersehen, zumal auch bei den anderen Kompanien noch Verwundete
wie Tote zu verzeichnen waren. –

Bei einer späteren Unterhaltung mit einem beteiligten Fliegeroffizier
dieser Gruppe, erzählte dieser: Die Fliegergruppe hatte den Auftrag,
zu einem festgesetzten Zeitpunkt den Hügel zur Unterstützung der
Kampfgruppe Kohlhaas mit Bomben zu belegen. Sie hielt es beim
Einfliegen für unmöglich, daß die Höhe bereits in eigener Hand war. –

Ritterkreuzträger des RAD

Arbeitsführer
Konopka
griff als Oberleutnant der
Reserve und Bataillons-

führer im Orelbogen mit
seinem Bataillon den stark
überlegenen Gegner an,
durchbrach dessen Stellung
und erbeutete mehrere
Geschütze. In entschlos-
sener Ausnutzung der da-
durch entstandenen gün-
stigen Lage setzte er sein
Bataillon zum erfolgreichen
Angriff auf eine beherr-
schende Höhe an und er-
möglichte dadurch dem
Regiment, von dort aus
am nächsten Tage den An-
griff fortzusetzen.

KRIEG, Gerhard, Master Sergeant
Assault Squadron Brigade 243 (FBB), Knight's
Cross 3/28/1945

With his assault gun, Master Sergeant Krieg
plugged a gaping hole in the front at Mande St.
Marie and Sibret on December 29, 1944, helf off
enemy tank attacks and splendidly supported the
hard-fighting units of the Führer Escort Brigade.

LANGE, Erhard, First Lieutenant
Defense Command BR, Knight's Cross 1/15/1943

Nearly five months—from August to December
of 1942—First Lieutenant Lange was the leader
of the "Schamil" operation with a special
command before the German lines in the
Caucasus area near Grossny, and returned with
the results of reconnaissance via dangerous
routes.

LARSDEN, Rudolf, Sergeant
I./Pz. Regiment GD, Knight's Cross 10/23/1944
During a large-scale Soviet attack on the Rozan bridgehead, Sergeant Larsen halted an enemy breakthrough with great bravery, destroying 52 enemy tanks and bringing his total score to 66 tanks.

LAU, Werner, Lieutenant
5th/Training Regiment BR zbV 800, Knight's Cross 12/9/1942
In an objective operation on October 9, 1942, carried out at platoon strength, Lieutenant Lau was able to capture the double bridge over the Terek at Arik unharmed. By neutralizing the explosive charges on the bridge, it could be kept open for the continued advance.

SS ECHO

1. Dezember 1942:
Abwehrkampf bei Olenin
Heldentod von Oberst Köhler,
Kommandeur Gren.-Rgt.

*

Der Führer verlieh das Ritterkreuz des Eisernen Kreuzes an Unteroffizier Rudolf Larsen im Panzer-Regiment.

Uffz. Larsen hat bisher 52 feindliche Panzer abgeschossen. Bei einem sowjetischen Großangriff im Brückenkopf Rozan hat er durch seine beispielhafte Tapferkeit einen Durchbruch stärkerer feindlicher Infanteriekräfte verhindert. Er blieb trotz stärkstem, auf seinen Panzer konzentrierten Pak- und Artilleriefeuer so lange in dem bedrohten Abschnitt der HKL, bis eigene Infanterie die Stellungen wieder besetzen konnte. Er verhinderte damit den sowjetischen Durchbruch durch die Ostpreußenstellung an der wichtigen Rollbahn Rozan—Ostenburg.

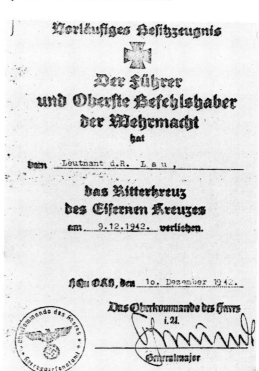

LEHNHOFF, Ernst-Günter, Major
Pz. Fusilier Battalion FGB, Knight's Cross
12/12/1944

Soviets fleeing back from the West on October 22, 1944 tried to escape encirclement via the Rominte bridge. The armored fusiliers, under the command of Major Lehnhoff, destroyed more than 30 enemy tanks and kept the river crossing in German hands.

LEIPZIG, Hellmut von, Lieutenant
Pz. A.A. BR, Knight's Cross 4/28/1945

Lieutenant von Leipzig and his men advanced in the area of Milkel Castle near Bautzen on April 24, 1945 and were able to drive the Soviets out of their positions. In bitter close combat, the surprised enemy was forced to withdraw, sustaining heavy losses.

Major Ernst Günter Lehnhoff
Kommandeur "Pz.Füs.Btl.(gep)
FGB

Gefecht bei DAKEN am 22.10.44   Ritterkreuz: 12.Dezember 1944

Seine spätere Ausrüstung und die sich in FALLINGBOSTEL ergebene Gliederung zeigt folgendes Bild:

Btl.-Stab - Kdr. Major L e h n h o f f
              Adj. Oblt. Krohn
              O.O. Lt. von Alvensleben,Lt.Mutius

1. -3.Schtz.Kp. mit : je 1 mittl.SPW als Chefwagen
                    : je 5 mittl.SPW mit 2-cm -Fla
                    : 22 mittl.SPW mit Bord-MG
4.(schw.)Kp.   : 28 mittl.SPW mit Wurfrahmen

Als Kp.-Chefs dieser Zeit sind zu nennen:
                    Hptm. Walter Ludwig
                    Oblt. Luchesi
                    Hptm. Lindemann
                    Oblt. Schubert

Nun - die Panzer-Abteilung F G B kann das fast eingeschlossene "Pz.Füs.Btl." nicht erreichen; sie rennt sich vielmehr in den nun nach Osten zurückflutenden Feind-Pz.-Rudeln fest und beisst sich den ganzen Tag westl. D A K E N in schweren Feuergefechten fest. Immer mehr feindl. Panzer werden abgeschossen, aber auch zahlreiche eigene gehen dabei verloren. Es ist ein schwerer Kampf der Besatzungen gegen die nun schon bekannten und überlegenen "Josef-Stalin"-Panzer mit ihren 12,2 -cm Kwk, die kaum und nur unter günstigsten Bedingungen überhaupt "geknackt" werden können.

Schliesslich gelingt es Teilen des "Pz.Füs.Btl.(gep.)" F G B unter Major L e h n h o f f bis nach GROSS'- TELLERODE, hart südl. GROSSWALTERSDORF, vorzustossen und den Brückenübergang über die " Rominte" zumindest durch Feuer zu sperren. Hier aber versuchen die aus Westen zurückflutenden Sowjets mit Panzern und Infanterie den Übergang zu erzwingen, um aus der Umklammerung herauszukommen. Es kommt zu verbissenen Nahkämpfen zwischen den Verteidigern und den zurückflutenden Sojets . Insgesamt werden in diesem Kampfgebiet mehr als 30 Fd.-Panzer vrrnichtet - der "Rominte"-Übergang aber bleibt in der Hand der Pz.-Füsiliere.Im Norden wird sich verstärkender Gefechtslärm vernehmbar, die dort angreifenden 5.Pz.Div. und Fallsch.Pz.Gren.Div.H G stossen nach Süden - auf GROSSWALTERSDORF zu."

entnommen: GD-Manu -S. 1074/75

Leutnant Hellmut von Leipzig
Fhr. in der "Pz.AA. BRANDENBURG

Gefecht bei MILKEL- 24.4.45   Ritterkreuz: 28.April 1 9 4 5

'" Auf dem Absetzungsweg Richtung BAUTZEN lagen wir bei MILKEL (nördl. BAUTZEN) in Reserve.
Der Jagdzug unter Leutnant von Leipzig alarmiert, nachdem der Gegner mit Panzerunterstützung einen Einbruch im Bereich des Schlosses MILKEL erzielt hatte.Es war gegen 1200 Uhr Mittags und die Sowjets machten sich zunächst über die Weinvorräte im Keller des Schlosses her.
Dieses ausnutzend - stiess von Leipzig mit seinen Fahrzeugen vor und konnte die Sowjets aus ihren Stellungen vertreiben.
Da bemerkte von Leipzig , dass der Gegner auch nördlich an einem Bach sich den eigenen Stellungen näherte - er stiess auch dagegen vor - und zwar in die Flanke der Angreifer (vermutlich Polen ?) - und in einem verbittert geführten Nahkampf die so überraschten Gegner so bedrängen, dass sie schliesslich unter erheblichen Verlusten in ihre Ausgangsstellungen zurückfluteten.
Leutnant von Leipzig hatte sich während dieses Gefechtes völlig verschossen und musste zur Pistole greifen.Im Nahkampf kämpfte er u.a. die Besatzung eines abgeschossenen Fd.-Panzers nieder.
Der Jagdzug hatte insgesamt 2 - 3 Verwundete, der Gegner liess an die 20 - 30 Gefallene zurück.""

entnommen: Brief-Bericht
Christian -Henrich Erb-
Prinz zu Stolberg-Wernigerode
vom 21.4.1981 - nach persönl.
Gespräch mit H.v.L. in Afrika

LEX, Hans, First Lieutenant
7th/Pz. Regiment GD, Knight's Cross 9/10/1943
First Lieutenant Lex destroyed 16 enemy tanks, without losses of his own, from a tank position near Novenskoje on July 15, 1943, through bravery and quick decisiveness, thus disposing of a strong flank threat.

LEYCK, Siegfried, Captain
III./Pz. Fusilier Regiment GD, Knight's Cross 12/17/1943
On July 4, 1943 armored fusiliers under the command of Captain Leyck launched a surprise attack at Gerzovka/Butovo, in order to attain better starting positions for the beginning of the attack on the next morning. While storming the enemy positions, Captain Leyck was severely wounded and succumbed on July 7, 1943.

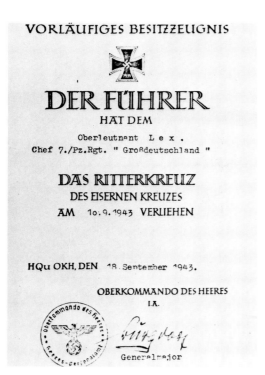

VORLÄUFIGES BESITZZEUGNIS

DER FÜHRER

HAT DEM

Oberleutnant Lex.
Chef 7./Pz.Rgt. " Großdeutschland "

DAS RITTERKREUZ

DES EISERNEN KREUZES

AM 1o.9.1943 VERLIEHEN

HQu OKH, DEN 18.September 1943.

OBERKOMMANDO DES HEERES
I.A.

Generalmajor

VORLÄUFIGES BESITZZEUGNIS

DER FÜHRER

HAT DEM

Hauptmann Leyck
Kdr. III./Füs.Rgt. Großdeutschland

DAS RITTERKREUZ

DES EISERNEN KREUZES

AM 17.12.1943 VERLIEHEN

HQu OKH, DEN 19.Dezember 1943.

OBERKOMMANDO DES HEERES
I.A.

Generalleutnant

LORENZ, Karl, Colonel
Pz. Grenadier Division GD, Knight's Cross
12/17/1942, Oak leaves (395.) 2/12/1944

At Wereista in the Lutschesa Valley on December 2, 1942 Major Lorenz was able, despite being wounded, to lead a battle group made up of support troops to make a successful counterattack to repulse a serious threat to the airstrip and thus hold his own HKL. The oak leaves to the Knight's Cross (395.) were awarded to Colonel Lorenz for a counterthrust made on November 17, 1943 at Krivoj Rog, on his own initiative and with one antitank gun and 15 men, in which several enemy tanks were destroyed and large numbers of infantry were driven back.

MAAZ, Heinz, Senior Corporal
3rd/Pz. A.A. GD, Knight's Cross 10/4/1944

In fighting off a Russian attack before Doblen on September 25, 1944, Senior Corporal Maaz stood firm at the head of his group in close combat, using well-aimed machine-gun fire to hold off the enemy, who was compelled to withdraw with heavy losses.

MADER, Hellmuth, Major General
Leader, Grenadier Division, Swords (143.) to oak
leaves of the Knight's Cross 4/18/1945
For his alert leadership of the Führer Grenadier
Division, which had to withstand the heaviest
offensive and defensive fighting near Lauban
between March 1 and 5, 1945, Major General
Mäder was decorated with the swords to the oak
leaves of the Knight's Cross.

MAGOLD, Hanns, First Lieutenant
1st/Assault Brigade GD, Knight's Cross 4/3/1943
In an attack on March 9, 1943 against Novy-
Mertshik, First Lieutenant Magold and his
assault-gun battery was detailed to a battle group
of the Panzer A.A. GD and scored great defensive
success. Seven enemy tanks and four guns, 37
antitank guns and much equipment were
destroyed.

Der Übergang über den Mok Mertschik-Bach ist schwierig, da
die Brücke völlig zerstört und das Eis infolge des Tauwetters
nicht mehr fest ist. – Endlich wird auch eine Umgehung gefunden,
doch leider ist ein Sturmgeschütz schon eingebrochen.
Die 4. Schwadron tritt darauf weiter an und greift über 199,3 den Ort
Grigorowka an. Auf den Höhen nördlich 188,7 werden flüchtende
feindliche Schlittenkolonnen ein rasches Opfer unserer Sturmgeschütze und 3,7-cm-Flak.
Aus Alexandrowka, das links von 188,7 im Tal liegt, erhalten die
vorgehenden Schwadronen Artillerie-Feuer, was zur Folge hat, daß
sich der inzwischen gebildete Fahrzeugpulk in alle Richtungen zerstreut. Die 2.(SPW)Schwadron stößt inzwischen auf Tarassowka
weiter vor, um sich dann gegen Bairak zu wenden.
Währenddessen greift die 3. Schwadron trotz des heftigen Gegen-
feuers in rücksichtslosem Zupacken von der Höhe herunter den Ort
Alexandrowka an und dringt, nachdem die Sturmgeschütze drei
unmittelbar am Ortsrand stehende 7,62-Pak erledigt haben, in den
Ort ein, wo es nochmals zu einem heftigen Häuserkampf kommt.
Der Stab steht währenddessen mit dem vorgesch. Beobachter der
Artillerie auf Höhe 188,7 und beobachtet, wie der Russe in dichten
Kolonnen mit Geschützen, Schlitten, LKW und sogar zwei Panzern aus
dem großen, nordwärts Alexandrowka leicht ansteigenden Wald flieht.
Für die Nacht beziehen die Schwadronen Sicherungen, und zwar die
2. (SPW) im Westteil Kirassirskij, die 3. (VW) Schwadron in Alexan-
drowka und die 4. (MG.)Schw. in Grigorowka. –
Ein sehr erfolgreicher Tag ist zu Ende gegangen; das beweisen die
Erfolgs- und Beutezahlen, nämlich: 7 Feind-Panzer vernichtet,
davon 3 T-34, 4 Feind-Geschütze 12,2-cm, einundzwanzig 7,62-Pak,
sechzehn 4,7-cm-Pak sowie zahlreiche Schlitten, Handwaffen, ein
Tornister-Funkgerät, Pz.-Büchsen usw. erbeutet. Etwa 300 Feindtote werden gezählt.
Gegen 2.10 Uhr geht beim Stab der verst. A.A. GD der Funkspruch
der Division ein, daß das verst. Füs.Rgt. GD ablösen und die Ab-
teilung in Kowjagi zur Verfügung sammeln solle." –
An den Erfolgen dieser im Verhältnis kleinen Kampfgruppe hat besonders auch die 1. Batterie/Stu.Gesch.Abt. GD unter Hauptmann
Magold teil, auf deren Konto der Abschuß der Mehrzahl der Feindpanzer
an diesem Tage und in diesem Abschnitt kommt.
Wegen dieser hervorragenden Leistungen wird Hptm. Magold zum
Ritterkreuz eingereicht.

GD-II. S.102

MATHEJA, Siegmund, Sergeant
1st Pz. Howitzer Unit FGD, Knight's Cross
5/6/1945

For disposing of six enemy tanks at the Bisamberg southeast of Korneuberg at the end of April 1945, Sergeant Matheja was awarded the Knight's Cross.

MOLLENDORFF, Leonhard von, Captain
III./Pz. Grenadier Regiment FBB, Knight's Cross
1/8/1945

In bitter close combat, the brave men of the III./Grenadier Regiment FBB, under the leadership of Captain von Möllendorff, destroyed American tanks that had broken into their own positions near Hubermont on January 1 and 2, 1945. During this hand-to-hand combat, Captain von Möllendorff was fatally wounded.

MULLER-ROCHHOLZ, Friedrich, Captain
Pz. Assault Engineer Battalion BR, Knight's
Cross 5/8/1945
The successful outbreak of the Assault Engineers
under the leadership of their Commander,
Captain Müller-Rochholz, from Niesky to
Rabenthal on April 21 and 22, 1945—taking with
them all of their wounded and numerous
refugees—saved not only the soldiers but also the
inhabitants from the Soviet attack.

NATZMER, Oldwig von, Lieutenant Colonel of
the General Staff
Infantry Division (motorized) GD, Knight's Cross
9/4/1943
When ordered on August 15, 1943 to take the
towns of Kusemin and Belsk, which were
occupied by the enemy, an armored battle group
under the command of the 1st General Staff
Officer of the I.D. GD attacked south of Achtyrka
and led the operation to a successful conclusion.

Ordensgemeinschaft
der Ritterkreuzträger des Eisernen Kreuzes e. V.
Orden vom Militär-Verdienst-Kreuz e. V.
Präsidiumsmitglied
VORSITZENDER DER ORDENSKOMMISSION
Walther-Peer Fellgiebel
Postfach 3689, Neue Krame 26/II, 6000 Frankfurt a. M.1, c/o DZMG
Telefon 0611/209 41

Herrn
Friedrich Müller-Rochholz   6000 Frankfurt a. M. 1, 16.6.1980
Kircheichstr. 126

5120 Herzogenrath Kohlscheid

E R K L Ä R U N G

Nach den mir vorliegenden Originalbriefen und Erklärungen hat
der Kommandeur der Pz.-Gren.Division "Brandenburg" General
Schulte-Heuthaus etwa zwischen Mitte und Ende März 1945 im
Verlauf der sehr schweren Abwehrkämpfe im Raume Görlitz, Weiss-
wasser, Bautzen und Königswartha 5 Soldaten seiner Division zur
Verleihung des Ritterkreuzes des Eisernen Kreuzes vorgeschlagen.

Unter diesen 5 Soldaten befanden sich u.a. die Majore Bröckerhoff
und Vosshage und der
        Kommandeur des Pionier-Bataillons der Division
        "Brandenburg" Hauptmann Friedrich Müller-Rochholz.

(Zeugen dafür sind der Erste Generalstabsoffizier der Division
Oberstleutnant i.G.a.D. Dr. jur. Johannes Erasmus und der IIa
der Division Major a.D. Werner Lau,nach Angaben in den Briefen des
Gen.Mj. Hermann Schulte-Heuthaus vom 4.5.1956 und 7.3.1961).

Der letzte Kommandierende General des Panzerkorps "Großdeutschland",
General der Panzertruppe a.D. Dr. Georg Jauer erklärte schriftlich am
29.3.1961, daß er Ordensanträge für verdiente Offiziere grundsätz-
lich positiv behandelte. Es heißt in der Erklärung weiter wörtlich:

        "Wenn dazu - wie im vorliegenden Fall - ein Divisions-
        Kommandeur von der Prägung eines Generals Schulte-Heuthaus
        einen solchen Antrag stellte, dann war mir das doppelter
        Anlaß zur Befürwortung."

Aufgrund dieser unmißverständlichen Erklärung und zahlreicher weiterer
Zusammenhänge - die hier aufzuführen entschieden zu weit führen wür-
de - steht eindeutig fest, daß der Vorschlag zur Verleihung des Ritterkreuzes
des Eisernen Kreuzes an den ehemaligen Hauptmann Friedrich Müller-
Rochholz, Kommandeur des Pionier-Bataillons der Division "Brandenburg" unter der Bestimmung des sogenannten Dönitz-Erlasses vom 7.5.1945
fällt und dementsprechend Herr Friedrich Müller-Rochholz sich recht-
mässig als Träger des Ritterkreuzes des Eisernen Kreuzes ausgeben kann.

Ungeachtet der Lage an der Stadtrandstellung von Achtyrka, die unter
dem Schutz starker eigener Artillerie gehalten werden kann, erteilt die
Division Befehl, alle gepanzerten Teile - dabei auch die I. (SFL) Abt./
Pz.Art.Rgt. GD und das I. (SPW) Btl./Pz.Gren.Rgt. GD mit Teilen -
in der Nacht 14./15. August herauszuziehen und westlich der Stadt zu
versammeln. Hinzu tritt die gerade mit Panzerteilen entladene III.
(Tiger) Abt./Pz.Rgt. GD unter Major Gomille sowie Masse der Pz.
Aufkl.Abt. GD. - Vorgesehener Plan: Versammlung noch während
der Nacht beiderseits Jassenowoje; mit Morgengrauen Antreten dieser
gepanzerten Gruppe unter Befehl des Ia, Obstlt. i. G. von Natzmer,
zum gewaltsamen Stoß nach Süden. Wegnahme der feindbesetzten
Orte Grun, Kusemin und Belsk, Vernichtung oder Vertreibung des
auf das Westufer der Worskla übergegangenen Feindes.
Während die Schwadronen der Pz.A.A. GD in den Orten Punkt 201,6,
Gnilza und Persche Trawnja sichern, die Batterien der Fla-Abt. 616
ihre Rohre gegen das feindbesetzte Dsjubi richten, rollt die „Kampfgruppe Natzmer" mit dem ersten Morgengrauen des 15. August nach
Süden an. Mit I. Abt. unter Mj. Pössel vornweg, die III. (Tiger) Abt.
hinterher, dabei die Schützenpanzer der I. (SPW) Btl./Pz.Gren., geht
der Vorstoß in Richtung Grun, während die 2. (SPW) Schwadron/
Pz.A.A. GD mit der Pz.Kp. Oblt. Lex den Weg unmittelbar ostwärts
der Rollbahn - also zwischen der Worskla und der Rollbahn - auf Budy
nimmt, wo sie sich mit der Masse der Kampfgruppe wieder vereinigen soll.
Trotz Minen und nicht unerheblicher Feindpak kann die Hauptgruppe
gegen 13.00 Uhr in Grun eindringen, wo noch mehrere feindliche
überschwere Sturmgeschütze mit 12,2-cm Kaliber vernichtet werden.
Dabei zeigt sich besonders die klare Überlegenheit der Tiger, die hier
ihre ersten Panzerkämpfe bestehen.
Doch unverzüglich geht es weiter, und gegen 15.00 Uhr kann die
verst. 2. (SPW) Schwadron, die vorübergehend bei Rybalske schwer zu
knacken hatte, in Budy das Zusammentreffen mit der Hauptgruppe melden.
Der unter Lt. Gebhard über Sinkiw, Dobshok auf Kusemin und Belsk
angesetzte Pz.-Spähtrupp berichtet, daß Feind in hellen Scharen nach
Süden fliehe.

GD- II -S.254

254

NEUMEYER, Werner, Lieutenant
I./Pz. Regiment 26 (GD), Knight's Cross
10/23/1944
On October 10, 1944 in the Krottingen area, Lieutenant Neumeyer, leading the way in his tank, wiped out six enemy tanks and, after the disabling of his tank, fought on as infantry with his crew.

NIEMACK, Horst, Colonel
Pz. Fusilier Regiment GD, Swords (69.) to the Knight's Cross 6/4/1944
On May 2, 1944 in the Targul Frumos area, the armored fusiliers under the command of Colonel Niemack proved to be tougher than 32 enemy tanks. The colonel, with a small group of determined men, threw themselves against the enemy tank attack and destroyed eight enemy tanks in close combat. The colonel was honored with the swords to the oak leaves of the Knight's Cross.

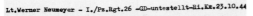

Lt.Werner Neumeyer – I./Pz.Rgt.26 –GD–untestellt–Ri.Kr.23.10.44

So besetzt die „Kampfgruppe Schwarzrock" (verst. Pz.Gren.Rgt.) die befohlene Widerstandslinie, während die „Kampfgruppe von Breese" (verst. Pz.Füs.Rgt. GD) über Plateliai – Salantai den Raum Krottingen zu erreichen sucht, wo die Pz.A.A. GD bereits mit den auf Krottingen stoßenden starken feindlichen Infanterie- und Panzer-Spitzen im Kampf steht. „Kampfgruppe von Breese" greift mit I. (SPW) und III. Btl. nach kurzer Bereitstellung in Richtung Raguviskiai an und vermag die gewonnene Linie entlang der Minia bis zum Abend zu halten.
Bei diesem Angriff unterstützt Lt. Neumeyer von der I./Pz.Rgt. 26 mit seinen 3 Panthern den Angriff des I. (SPW) Btl./Pz.Füs. Nach dem Feuerschlag der Artillerie – III. Abteilung – fährt Neumeyer aus eigenem Entschluß in schneidiger Fahrt den Schützenpanzerwagen voraus und vernichtet auf Anhieb insgesamt 6 Feind-Panzer. Durch diesen Erfolg wird das nachfolgende SPW-Bataillon in einen zügigen Angriff gerissen. – Im weiteren Verlauf wird der Panther des Leutnants als vorderster Panzer durch Treffer im Laufwerk unbeweglich geschossen. Im anhaltenden Feuer von vier feindlichen Pak und mehreren Feind-Panzern bekämpft er den Gegner frei im Gelände stehend und schießt weitere zwei Feind-Panzer, 2 Pak und 7 LKW zusammen. Während-dessen erhält sein unbeweglich stehender Panzer Treffer auf Treffer. Aber er bootet nicht aus, sondern kämpft weiter. Schließlich durch-schlägt der 9. Treffer seinen Panzer und verletzt Neumeyer an beiden Oberschenkeln. Kaum in ein anderes Fahrzeug umgestiegen, schießt er nochmals zwei Feind-Panzer zusammen und wird wiederum abge-schossen. Wieder bootet er aus und kämpft zusammen mit seiner Besatzung mit den Pz.-Füsilieren infanteristisch weiter. Dieser persön-liche und auf den Angriff sich hervorragend auswirkende Einsatz des Lt. Neumeyer wird später durch die Verleihung des Ritterkreuzes

GD-Bd.II-S.641

Oberst N I E M A C K erhielt die Schwerter.

F"hrerhauptquartier, 6.6.1944.

Der F"hrer verlieh am 4. Juni das Eichenlaub mit Schwertern zum Ritterkreuz des Eisernen Kreuzes an Oberst Horst Niemack, Kommandeur eines Panzerf"silierregiments, als 69. Soldaten der deutschen Wehr-macht.

Zu Beginn des Feldzuges gegen die Sowjetunion hatte der damalige Rittmeister mit seiner Aufklärungsabteilung maßgeblichen Anteil an der raschen Erzwingung des Njemen"berganges.
Am 2. Mai 1944 trat der Feind östlich des Sereth zum entscheidungs-suchenden Angriff an. Das Panzerf"silierregiment "Großdeutschland" unter seinem Kommandeur Oberst Niemack hielt dem feindlichen Ansturm stand. Eine Gruppe von 34 schweren und schwersten Kampfwagen tauchte plötzlich vor dem Gefechtsstand des Obersten Niemack auf und bedrohte eine wichtige Querstraße. Oberst Niemack hatte nur seinen Stab, den Nachrichtenzug und einige Fahrer zur Ver f"gung. An der Spitze dieser kleinen Schar warf er sich dem Feind entgegen. In erbittertem Nahkam wurden acht Panzer vernichtet, der Regimentskommandeur war die Seele des Widerstandes und erledigte persönlich den sowjetischen Befehls-panzer mit dem Kommandeur des ganzen Verbandes. Damit war der Angriff an dieser Stelle abgewiesen.

214

NUHN, Heinrich, Captain
Pz. Engineer Battalion FGD, Knight's Cross
5/9/1945
Captain Nuhn and his armored engineers took a
major part in the recapture of Deutsch-Wagram
on April 10, 1945. In the following days they
fought off repeated enemy tank attacks near
Gerastorf in bitter fighting.

OESTERWITZ, Karl Heinz, Lieutenant Colonel
Jäger Regiment 2 BR, Knight's Cross 4/30/1943,
oak leaves (734.) 2/10/1945
In the "classic Brandenburg way", First
Lieutenant Oesterwitz captured a bridge at
Beloretschkaya in zbV action on August 11, 1942,
after fighting his way through the Soviet bridge
defenses with a camouflaged Russian truck.
Lieutenant Colonel Oesterwitz was honored with
the oak leaves to the Knight's Cross for freeing a
German supply train with fuel, ammunition and
supplies from a town already occupied by the
Russians and leading it back to the German lines
in the Sprottau area on February 11 and 12, 1945.

Ordensgemeinschaft
der Ritterkreuzträger des Eisernen Kreuzes e. V.
Orden vom Militär-Verdienst-Kreuz e. V.

Freie Mitglied
VORSITZENDE DER ORDENSKOMMISSION
Walther-Peer Fellgiebel
Postfach 2689, Neue Kräme 26/II, 6000 Frankfurt a. M. 1, c/o DZMG
Telefon 0611/20941

Bestätigung

6000 Frankfurt a. M. 1, 23.10.1980

Herrn Oberstleutnant a.D. Heinrich Nuhn, wohnhaft Wolfram-von-
Eschenbach-Str. 11, 6200 Wiesbaden, Tel.Nr. 06121/89467, wurde
das Ritterkreuz des Eisernen Kreuzes verliehen.

Der Vorschlag zur Verleihung des Ritterkreuzes des Eisernen
Kreuzes wurde ordnungsgemäß auf dem Dienstweg mit den er-
forderlichen Befürwortungen der Zwischenvorgesetzten weiter-
geleitet.

Dieser Vorschlag ist Ende April 1945 im Original beim OKH/PA/
P5 - Heerespersonalamt/Ordensabteilung - eingegangen und wurde
ordnungsgemäß in dem offiziellen Vorschlagbuch eingetragen.
Dem Vorschlag sind keinerlei Ablehnungsnotizen oder sonstige
zurückstellende Hinweise beigefügt.

Daraus ergibt sich eindeutig, daß der Vorschlag zur Verleihung
vorgesehen war, aber nicht mehr zur Erledigung kam.

Der letzte Reichspräsident, unser Ehrenmitglied, Herr Großadmiral
Karl Dönitz, hat uns schriftlich bestätigt, daß er Anfang Mai
1945 die Weisung erteilt hat, daß die bis zur Kapitulation am
8. Mai 1945 vorliegenden befürwortenden Vorschläge zur Verleihung
des Ritterkreuzes des Eisernen Kreuzes und höherer Stufen dieses
Ordens zu genehmigen seien. In der präzisierten schriftlichen
Äußerung des Großadmirals heißt es, daß die Voraussetzungen für
die Anerkennung der Verleihung ein ordnungsgemäß befürworteter
Vorschlag, ein rechtzeitiger Eingang beim Heerespersonalamt und
die entsprechende Eintragung im Vorschlagbuch waren.

Diese Voraussetzungen liegen im Falle des Oberstleutnant a.D.
Heinrich Nuhn ohne jeden Zweifel vor.

Herr Heinrich Nuhn ist danach Träger des Ritterkreuzes des Eisernen
Kreuzes und wird als solcher in unseren Unterlagen geführt.

F.d.R.

Walther-Peer Fellgiebel
Präsidialmitglied
Vorsitzender der Ordenskommission

PLICKAT, Fritz, Sergeant
II./Pz. Grenadier Regiment GD, Knight's Cross
12/9/1944
During the outbreak from Luoke on October 6, 1944, Sergeant Plickat and his antitank platoon destroyed four enemy tanks. Despite sustaining three wounds, he was able to break out to the west with his men.

POHLMANN, Wilhelm, Captain
Battle Group FBB, Knight's Cross 3/14/1943
The Pohlmann Battle Group/FBB war deployed during the winter battles of December 1942 and January 1943 to close a gaping hole in the front. In mid-January 1943 this battle group broke out of an encirclement and reached Starobyelsk.

```
                    Hauptmann Wilhelm Pohlmann
                    Führer:"Kampfgruppe Pohlmann"
            19.12.42 des:"Führer-Begleit-Bataillon"
Gefecht bei TSCHERTKOWO 15. 1.43  Ritterkreuz: 14.März 1 9 4 3

"Die am 13.Jan.1943 begonnene russ. Offensive hatte Inzwischen
eine Lücke von über 350 km in die Front der deutschen und ver-
bündeten Armeen gerissen.Die deutsche 2.Armee ist schwer angeschl
agen, mit der ungar. 2.Armee kann überhaupt nicht gerechnet wer-
den . Das in ihrem Abschnitt eingesetzte deutsche Armeekorps
weicht kämpfend auf den "Oskol" aus. Auch Reste des ital.Alpini
Korps und das XXIV.Pz.Korps sind nicht mehr verwandungsfähig,
und suchen nach Westen durchzukommen. Aus dem Raum beiderseits
STAROBJELSK kämpfen sich zwei deutsche Pz.-Divisionen und eine
Infanterie-Division mit offener Nordflanke gegen weit überlegenen
Feind auf KUPJANSK zurück.-
Die "Kampfgruppe P o h l m a n n " ( Teile:Fü,Begl.Btl.), eine d
ersten GD-Verbände, wird in den bedrohten Raum verlegt.Sie ist
kräftemässig schwach- 1 x Schtz., 1 x Pz.Kp.- allerddings vor-
züglich ausgerüstet. + 4.(schw.)Kp.
Im Eisentransport geht die Kampfgruppe in Marsch, wird jedoch
bereits auf dem Bahnweg " auseinandergerissen. Teile werden
südwestl. WORONESH ausgeladen - die Pz.Kp. und ein Fla-Zug lande
in TSCHWERTKOWO an der "Kalitwa"-
diese " abgespaltene" Gruppe kämpf künftig im Rahmen einer Kampf
gruppe Schulte, einer Rgt.-Einheit der 298.I.D.- die sich als
wandernder Kessel nach Westen durchschlagen will. Diese Kampfgru
pe zusammen mit den Teilen der Gruppe Pohlmann - werden dann im
Ort TSCHERTKOWO eingeschlossen, es ist der erste Weihnachtstag.
In den Nächsten Tagen toben schwerste Kämpfe um die Stadt TSCHER
KOWO, die an Opfern viele der tapferen Männer kostet.Aber es
wird gehalten.
Bei einem Ausbruchsversuch , die von der 5.(Pz.)Kp. der Gruppe
Pohlmann angeführt wird - fallen der Chef Oblt. Kegel und ein
Zugführ. , Lt. Wilkens (1.Jan.43)
Erst um den 15.Jan-1943 - als die Entlastungstruppe - 19.P.D.
in der Nähe steht - erfolgt erneuter Ausbruchsversuch - der wie-
derum von den wenigen noch vorhandenen Panzer der 5.(Pz.)Kp.Poh
mann angeführt wird. Der Durchbruch zielt in Richtung STRICHAWK
wo sie von der "Sturmgeschütz-Lehr-Abteilung Jüterbog" aufgenomm
men wird.
Am 19.Jan.43 gelingt schliesslich die Wiedervereinigung mit den
Restteilen Pohlmann in STAROBJELSK.
entnommen: GD-Manu-S. 527/529
```

POSCHUSTA, Leopold, Sergeant
2nd/Pz. Fusilier Regiment GD, Knight's Cross
11/12/1943
Near Kommunar in the Krivoj Rog area on
October 6, 1943, Sergeant Poschusta made the
decision to attack an enemy preparation that
threatened a German airstrip. In hard fighting he
was able to throw back the Soviets and keep the
airstrip free.

POSSL, Walter, Major
I./Pz. Regiment GD, Knight's Cross 4/20/1943
Without sustaining any losses, the men of the
I./Panzer Unit GD, under the leadership of
Major Pössl, destroyed 39 T-34 tanks in hard
fighting east of Borrisovka on March 14, 1943
and prevented a dangerous flank attack on the
head of the Panzer A.A. GD.

PROHASKA, Ernst, Lieutenant
8th/Training Regiment BR zbV 800, Knight's
Cross 9/16/1942

On August 9, 1942, Lieutenant Prohaska and his Brandenburgers, in camouflaged action, stormed the Byelaya bridge at Maikop, destroyed the ignition cables, fought off the defenders with hand grenades and machine pistols, and formed a bridgehead. In this close combat Lieutenant Prohaska met his death.

RAMPEL, Josef, Sergeant
11th/Pz. Regiment GD, Knight's Cross
12/15/1943

Within 90 minutes at Taranzoff on October 18, 1943, despite damage to his own Tiger tank, Sergeant Rampel destroyed 17 enemy tanks that had tried to break through the German positions. A barracks building at the Munster Bundeswehr base was named after this brave soldier.

Neue Ritterkreuzträger

Führerhauptquartier, 4. Januar

Der Führer verlieh das Ritterkreuz des Eisernen Kreuzes an Oberstleutnant Ernst-Joachim B r a d e l, Kommandeur eines Panzergrenadier-Regiments; Leutnant Heinrich N i e d e r m e i e r, Zugführer in einem Gebirgsjäger-Bataillon; Oberfeldwebel Josef R a m p e l, Halbzugführer im Panzer-Regiment „Großdeutschland"; Obergefreiten Wilhelm S c h l e e t, Maschinengewehr-Schütze in einem Panzergrenadier-Regiment.

RANTZAU, Hans-Friedrich Count zu, Captain
I. (Pz. Howitzer)/Armored Artillery Regiment
GD, Knight's Cross 6/9/1944

During a Soviet attack at Kwitka on March 11,
1944, the Count used his guns to fight off the
Russians and led his men forward in infantry
action, stormed the town, took considerable
booty and, thanks to his bravery, prevented his
own defense front from being torn apart.

REMER, Otto Ernst, Major
I./Pz. Grenadier Regiment GD, Knight's Cross
5/18/1943, oak leaves (325.) 11/12/1943

At the head of his grenadiers, Major Remer
achieved great success at Kharkov in early
February of 1943. He proved to be a steadfast
commander who knew how to lead his men. He
was the 325th soldier of the German Wehrmacht
to be decorated with the oak leaves to the
Knight's Cross for outstanding leadership on the
Dniepr front in mid-1943.

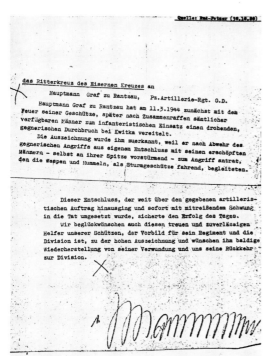

RIEDMULLER, Adam, Sergeant
2nd/Pz. Jäger Unit Kurmark, Knight's Cross
2/8/1945

Sergeant Riedmüller destroyed four Russian T-34 tanks at Kunersdorf on February 2, 1945, climbed out of his tank and destroyed two more Soviet tanks with his Panzerfaust.

ROGER, Hans, Sergeant
1st/Pz. Fusilier Regiment GD, Knight's Cross
9/21/1944

In an advance on the road to Kursenai on August 17, 1944 Sergeant Röger surprised a Russian 15-cm howitzer, attacked lightning-fast with the men of his platoon, drove off the accompanying Russian soldiers with machine-pistol fire, and captured the gun.

Der Kampfgruppen-Kommandeur Oberst Langkeit hat sich die Argumente seiner Kommandeure angehört und gibt nun den Ausbruchsbefehl – klar und sachlich. Der Angriff soll in den frühesten Morgenstunden entlang der Straße mit den wenigen noch verfügbaren Panzern von Major Hudel erfolgen. Doch der Versuch mißlingt.

Das I. Btl./Pz.Gren.Rgt. unter Major Petereit greift daraufhin erneut rechts der Straße (nach NW) in den Wald hinein an, um den dort immer wieder flankierend wirkenden Gegner zum Schweigen zu bringen. In schwerem Nahkampf gelingt es Petereit, sich dort mit seinen Männern festzusetzen, das Waldstück zu säubern und damit die Flankierung auszuschalten.

Die Hetzer der Jagdpanzer-Kompanie werden nun nach vorn gezogen, Hudel greift ebenfalls entlang der Straße an – und endlich, endlich gegen 14.00 Uhr ist der Gegner geworfen! Die ersten Fahrzeuge an der Spitze der Kolonne fahren, den Panzern folgend auf Kunersdorf zu. Dort kommt es an einem Panzer-Riegel der Sowjets noch einmal zu einem kurzen Feuergefecht, bei dem sich Feldwebel Riedmüller durch Abschuß von 4 T-34 besonders auszeichnet. Als er mit seinem Hetzer die anderen T-34 wegen des ungünstigen Geländes nicht erreichen kann, steigt er kurz entschlossen aus seinem Panzer und vernichtet zwei weitere mit der Panzer-Faust. Für diese Tat wird er mit dem Ritterkreuz ausgezeichnet.

Immer mehr Fahrzeuge rollen nun durch Kunersdorf, am Flugplatz vorbei in die Vorstadt Frankfurts ein. Das II. Btl./Pz.Gren.Rgt. bezieht zunächst Flankenstellungen in Kunersdorf, während die· Artillerie sofort Stellungswechsel bis an die ersten Häuser Frankfurts macht, um von dort aus die Bewegungen artilleristisch zu überwachen. Die Masse der Kampfgruppe Langkeit jedoch zieht zunächst in der Damm-vorstadt Frankfurt unter, gliedert neu, sammelt und verlegt dann auf das West-Ufer in die Kasernen an der Ausfall-Straße nach Westen. Lediglich das II. Btl./Pz.Gren.Rgt., die Art.Abt. Buboltz, die 11. (IG.) Kp. verbleiben noch auf dem Ostufer der Stadt und halten einen Brückenkopf um die Damm-Vorstadt, die laufend ihre Verstärkung durch Festungstruppen aus Frankfurt erhält.

III Großdeutschland 20

331

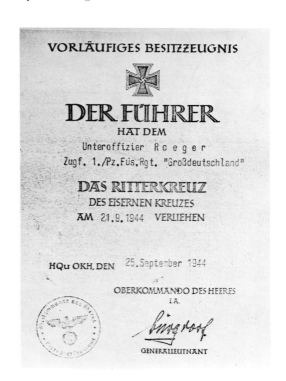

VORLÄUFIGES BESITZZEUGNIS

DER FÜHRER

HAT DEM

Unteroffizier Roeger
Zugf. 1./Pz.Füs.Rgt. "Großdeutschland"

DAS RITTERKREUZ
DES EISERNEN KREUZES
AM 21.9.1944 VERLIEHEN

HQu OKH, DEN   25.September 1944

OBERKOMMANDO DES HEERES
I.A.

GENERALLEUTNANT

ROSSMANN, Emil, Lieutenant
I./Pz. Regiment 26 (GD), Knight's Cross
10/23/1944

Although Lieutenant Rossmann and his panzer unit were encircled at Tryskiai on October 6, 1944, he made the decision to break out. In the process he destroyed six enemy T-34 tanks and 21 enemy antitank guns and drove the enemy to flight, without losing any of his own men.

ROTHKIRCH UND TRACH, H. S., Count von, Captain
I./Pz. Regiment 26 (GD), Knight's Cross
10/4/1944

In the Schaulen area on August 17, 1944. the Count and his tank unit, subordinate to the Panzergrenadier Division GD, destroyed nine enemy tanks and numerous antitank guns—although his unit had only six operable tanks. On his own initiative, he penetrated deep into the Soviet positions and thus opened the way for the grenadiers to continue the attack.

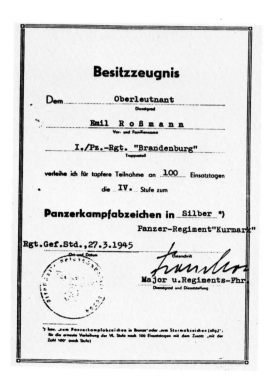

ROSEKE, Erich, First Lieutenant
6th/Jäger Regiment 1 BR, Knight's Cross
4/8/1945

As battalion leader, First Lieutenant Röseke held
the Apatin bridgehead in November of 1944 in
hard defensive fighting against the Soviets who
had crossed the Danube. Through his steadfastness he prevented their immediate further
penetration to the west.

SACHS, Hans, Senior Corporal
5th/Pz. Fusilier Regiment GD, Knight's Cross
9/10/1944

In September of 1944, Senior Corporal Sachs and
his group fought on the front at Doblen and
attacked a Soviet gathering on his own initiative.
With determination he pushed farther forward
and was able to capture numerous grenade
launchers and machine guns. He fought off a
Russian counterattack and held his position.

Über seine Tat, die ebenfalls zur Auszeichnung mit dem Ritterkreuz führte,
berichtet der Obergefreite Hans Sachs von der 5. Kp./Pz.Füs.Rgt. GD:

„Während unser 1. Btl. weit nach Osten vorgestoßen war, hatten
wir den Auftrag, die Sowjets, die sich noch in den Wäldern festgesetzt hatten, zu vernichten. Als ich mit meiner Gruppe in Stellung
ging, entdeckte ich, wie sich drüben Infanteristen und Panzer bereit-
stellten. Da habe ich nicht lange überlegt. Nichts wie ran, und dann
stürmten wir mit Hurra in den Iwan hinein. Es gab ein wüstes Durch-
einander, aber wir ließen uns nicht verblüffen.

Ein Panzer wurde durch einen meiner Kameraden im Nahkampf
vernichtet; aber wieviele Sowjets wir eigentlich umgelegt hatten,
das war in der Eile gar nicht festzustellen. Die Gelegenheit ist günstig,
dachte ich, und so stießen wir weiter und trafen – ohne uns um die
Iwans noch viel zu kümmern – auf eine Nachschubkolonne, prima
Studebakers!

Wieder erledigten wir 15 Sowjets im Nahkampf und machten reiche
Beute an Munition und Verpflegung. Von Gefangenen erfuhren wir,
daß es nicht mehr weit zu den Trossen sei. Ich ließ meine Männer an
einer Wegegabelung in Stellung gehen und arbeitete mich selbst vor,
um zu sehen, was los war.

Ich kam nicht weit, denn plötzlich rauschte eine volle sowjetische
Kompanie auf unsere Stellungen zu. Rankommen lassen, dachte ich
noch, und dann hinein!!

Und dann kam alles so schnell, daß gar keine Zeit mehr zum Nach-
denken war.

Als wir schließlich den letzten Schuß abgegeben hatten und uns endlich mal umsehen konnten, fanden wir mindestens 25 Gefallene,
18 Verwundete, zwei Granatwerfer, ein s.MG., drei l.MG. und viele
Gewehre und Pistolen.

SOMMER, Clemens, Major
II./Pz. Grenadier Regiment GD, Knight's Cross
1/18/1945
In order to free an enclosed group near Luoke on
October 6, 1944, a battle group of Panzergrenadier
Regiment GD under Major Sommer was
deployed. In man-to-man combat the breakout
from Luoke could be accomplished with support
from three of their own tanks.

SPAETER, Helmuth, Captain
2nd/Pz. A.A. GD, Knight's Cross 7/28/1943
Disregarding heavy enemy flank fire from the
Kubassovsky Ravine, Captain Spaeter decided on
June 10, 1943 to fling his squadron into the flank
of the advancing Soviets. He drove back the hard-
fighting enemy, destroyed six enemy tanks, took
many prisoners and captured much materiel.

SCHEUNEMANN, Kurt, Sergeant
2nd/Pz. Regiment FBB, Kinght's Cross 1/8/1945
Within five minutes on December 24, 1944
Sergeant Scheunemann was able, during the
Ardennes offensive in the St. Vith area, to destroy
five enemy tanks and two guns and thus break the
enemy's resistance.

SCHMIDT, Erich, Lieutenant Colonel
Pz. Regiment FGD, Oak leaves (877.) to the
Knight's Cross 5/9/1945
Around April 12, 1945 Lieutenant Colonel
Schmidt led a mixed armored group in a night
attack on an enemy position near Raasdorf and
destroyed many enemy tanks. Enemy attempts to
achieve a breakthrough could be prevented for
the time being.

berichtet: Kt.Scheunemann persönl. 16.Feb.1981: aus:Canada
================================== ==================================
"Am 23. und 24.Dezmber 1944 wurde ich mit meinem Zug einer Vorau
Abteilung zugeteilt.Wenn ich mich recht erinnere, war es die
"Kradschtz.-Abteilung" der Fü.Begl.Brig.-
Nach anfänglich gutem Vormarsch auf der Strasse kam der Vor-
marsch zum Halten. Der Ruf " Feindpanzer !" vorne - kam durch.
Beim Vorziehen zur Spitze stellte ich fest, dass die anderen
Panzer unterwegs ausgefallen waren — Schnee,Glätte,Kälte....
     An der Spitze erklärte mir ein Offizier die Lage. Sie hatte
ziemliche Verluste durch Feindpanzer und wurden von schweren
Fd.-Panzern gestoppt.
Unter feindl. Beschuss und ohne Feuerschutz fuhr ich weiter
vor und konnte bald zwei schwere Fd.-Panzer ausmachen, die auf
uns schossen.Nach einigen eigenen Schüssen auf die feindl. Pan
zer fing der eine an zu brennen. Nach weiteren Schüssen auch
der Andere. Dann unter Deckung der brennenden Panzer fuhr ich
an diese heran.Die Strasse war dadurch gesperrt.
In einiger Entfernung sehe und höre ich — da wir den Motor ab-
gestellt hatten — Fahrzeug- und Panzer-Bewegungen. Auf diese
eröffnete ich das Feuer. Dabei schossen wir abwechseln Panzer-
und Sprenggranaten, auf nicht klar erkennbare Ziele.Das fein
Feuer liess jetzt nach und hörte bald ganz auf.
Mittlerweile waren auch die Kradschützen und ein eigener Panzer von mir nach vorn gekommen.
Zufuss ging ich dann mit dem Führer und einigen Leuten des
Krad-Zuges zu den abgeschossenen Fd.-Panzern und Fahrzeugen.
Ich war sehr überrascht, sovile Fd.-Panzer mit laufendem Mo-
tor zu sehen. Nach kurzer Zeit kamen auch die ersten Fd.-Be-
satzungen der Fahrzeuge aus dem Wald. Sie ergaben sich ohne
Widerstand.
Mein Kp.-Chef war plötzlich auch da und gratulierte mir zu dem
Erfolg.Wir hatten keine Verluste.— "
────────────────
persönl.Bericht K.Sch.

SCHNAPPAUF, Georg, Lieutenant Colonel
Pz. Regiment FBD, Knight's Cross 4/19/1945
With a battle group of the Panzer Regiment of
the Führer Escort Division, Lieutenant Colonel
Schnappauf was able to score important defensive
success in the Kamenz area in Saxony toward the
end of April 1945.

SCHONE, Hans-Wolfgang, First Lieutenant
II./Ensign Regiment 1242, Knight's Cross
3/23/1945
With an ensign battalion subordinate to the
Panzergrenadier Division Kurmark, First
Lieutenant Schöne was above to stand fast in
March of 1945 and prevent the Russians from
breaking through near Podelzig on the Oder.

SCHROEDTER, Erich, Captain
Pz. Reconnaissance Unit, GD, Knight's Cross
10/23/1944, oak leaves (808.) 3/28/1945
On October 5, 1944 the Panzer Reconnaissance
Unit GD advanced out of a bridgehead at
Tulkinciai into a Soviet position, freed an
encircled group and held the position despite
Russian attempts to surround him. In mid-
February 1945 the reinforced Panzer Recon-
naissance Unit GD, under Captain Schroedter,
fought at Pettelkau on the Passarge against a
Soviet armored brigade. It destroyed ten enemy
tanks and could hold the crossing free for a long
time.

SCHULTE, Hubert, Captain
I./Pz. Grenadier Regiment FBD, Knight's Cross
4/30/1945
After the battalion commander fell, Captain
Schulte took command of the armored grenadiers
and was able to break through successfully to
Arnswalde, Pomerania on February 15, 1945.

VORLÄUFIGES BESITZZEUGNIS

DER FÜHRER

HAT DEM

Rittmeister S c h r o e d t e r ,
Kommandeur Pz.Aufkl.Abt. "GD"

DAS RITTERKREUZ
DES EISERNEN KREUZES
AM 23.10.1944 VERLIEHEN

HQu OKH, DEN 30.10.1944

OBERKOMMANDO DES HEERES
I.A.

GENERALLEUTNANT

Hauptmann Hubert S c h u l t e
Btl.Fhr. I./Pz.Gr.Rgt. "Fü.Bgl.Div.
Gefecht bei ARNSWALDE-15.2.45   Ritterkreuz: 30.April 1 9 4 5

Hauptm. S c h u l t e , der nach der Verwundung von Hptm.Störck
die Führung des I./Pz.Gren.Rgt. Fü.Begl.Div. übernommen hatte,
stiess nach Südosten auf ARNSWALDE vor.
" Die Chaussee von MARIENBERG nach ARNSWALDE war für die Fahrzeuge
kaum passierbar, denn die grossen Strassenbäume waren sämtlich ab-
gesägt und lagen quer und sperrig auf der Fahrbahn. Unsere Wagen
mieden die unbequeme Strasse und fuhren neben ihr stadteinwärts.
Hinter dem Ersten Haus am Ortseingang begrüssten uns freudig und
mit erhobenen Händen die Sicherungsposten der "Kampfgruppe Voigt".
(Dr.Tuchen).
Etwa 10 SPW rollten ohne Aufenthalt in die Innenstadt (von ARNS-
WALDE) und hielten in der Mühlenstrasse , vor der Ecke zum Markt."
(Dr.Tuchen). D a m i t war die erste Verbindung der Angriffstrup-
pen mit der "Kampfgruppe Voigt" hergestellt worden. Teile des
I./Pz.Gren.Rgt. F.B.D. hatten ihren Auftrag , blitzschnell nach
ARNSWALDE durchzustossen , in einem einmalig schneidigen gefah-
renen und riskanten Angriff durchgeführt. (Mörke-Bericht:S.37/38

Fest steht , dass der Einschliessungsring um ARNSWALDE am 15.Feb.
gesprengt wurde. Dies wird von den Teilnehmern Dr.Tuchen und Hptm.
Störck (FBD) bestätigt, der nach der Soldbucheintragung auch am
15.2.45 verwundet wurde.
Der Auftrag zum blitzschnellen Durchstoss bis ARNSWALDE war von
dem neuen Btl.-Kdr. - Hptm. S c h u l t e - mit etwa 10 SPW durchgeführt worden. (Mörke-Bericht: S. 39)

entnommen: Bericht Fritz Mörke
3340 Wolfenbüttel vom: 1962

SCHWARZROCK, Rudolf, Major
I./Pz. Grenadier Regiment GD, Knight's Cross
8/19/1944

Despite sustaining six wounds and losing his left leg, Major Schwarzrock fought along with his armored grenadier battalion at Tragul Frumos and Sereth in the first days of May 1944, gaining success against the Soviets and setting a splendid example of devotion to duty.

STEIDL, Konrad, Captain
I./2nd Regiment Division BR, Knight's Cross
1/26/1944

In withering defensive fire, First Lieutenant Steidl and his men stormed the Lim bridge in Prijepolje on December 3, 1943, stormed on against the barracks and finally broke all resistance. In the evening of the same day, the west bank was in German hands.

Aus dem Danziger Vorposten (Ende August 1944.):

Der Führer hat Major Udo Schwarzrock aus Danzig - Langfuhr das Ritterkreuz des Eisernen Kreuzes verliehen.
Dieser tapfere Offizier führt sein Bataillon im Panzergrenadier-Regiment "Großdeutschland" nach sechsmaliger Verwundung und Verlust de linken Beins, sodaß er gezwungen ist, sich am Stock zu bewegen. Seit März 1942 trägt er bereits das Deutsche Kreuz in Gold.
Als die Sowjets Anfang Mai 1944 an der rumänischen Front zum Groß angriff antraten und zwischen Targul Frumos und dem Sereth einen Einbruch erzielten, riß Major Schwarzrock kampfunerfahrende Männer in der Abwehr durch sein Beispiel in schwungvollem Gegenstoß vor wärts und warf die eingebrochenen Bolschewisten aus der Stellung. Am nächsten Tage rollten nach stundenlangem Trommelfeuer sowjetische Panzer an. Ihnen trat Major Schwarzrock mit zwei Pak und einem Infanteriegeschütz entgegen und vernichtete fünf schwere Panzer. Ein weiterer wurde durch Nahkampfmittel erledigt. Obwohl neue Panzer-wellen folgten, führte Major Schwarzrock seine Kampfgruppe planmäßig und geordnet in eine vorbereitete Auffangstellung, wobei er selbst stets bei der Nachhut blieb. Als die Bolschewisten auf dem linken Flügel eine wichtige Höhe in Besitz nehmen wollten, bzw. nahmen, gewann Major Schwarzrock mit den letzten Reserven die Höhe zurück. Dann hielt er die Stellung solange, bis durch heranrückende Truppen die Lücke auf dem linken Flügel wieder geschlossen und damit die Gefahr eines Durchbruchs beseitigt werden konnte. Bei diesem Kampf wurde Major Schwarzrock noch zwei Mal verwundet, gab aber die Führung der Truppe nicht ab, bis jede Gefahr beseitigt war.

Aus dem Tagesbefehl des Kommandeurs der Panzergrenadierdivision "Großdeutschland" am 22.8.1944. (Auszug aus dem G.D.-Echo.):

Der Führer verlieh das Ritterkreuz des Eisernen Kreuzes an Major Schwarzrock, Panzergrenadier - Regiment.
Major Schwarzrock hat sich in besonderem Maße in den überaus schweren, aber erfolgreichen Abwehrkämpfen der Division zwischen Targul Frumos und dem Sere th durch besondere Krisenfestigkeit und vorbildliche Führung ausgezeichnet.
Trotz schwerster Verwundungen hat dieser Offizier in treuester soldatischer Pflichterfüllung sich immer wieder zum Fronteinsatz gedrängt. Seine Energie, seine Einsatzbereitschaft und sein mitreissendes Vorbild sind den Männern des Panzergrenadier- als auch des Panzerfüsilier-Regiments ein Begriff.

(Gen. von Manteuffel)

STORCK, Georg, Captain
I.(SPW)/Pz. Grenadier Regiment FBD, Oak
leaves (880.) 5/9/1945

On February 15, 1945 Captain Störck and his
SPW battalion penetrated Soviet positions before
Arnswalde, Pomerania and was able to break
through to the city 12 km away. Despite severe
wounds, he entered the city and was able to free
many soldiers, wounded men and civilians.

STRACHWITZ VON GROSS-ZAUCHE UND
CAMMINETZ, Count Hyazinth, Colonel
Pz. Regiment GD, Swords (27.) to oak leaves of
the Knight's Cross 3/28/1943

For his action and the destruction of 154 enemy
tanks near Kharkov in February of 1943, the
"Armored Count" was decorated with the swords
(27th) to the oak leaves.

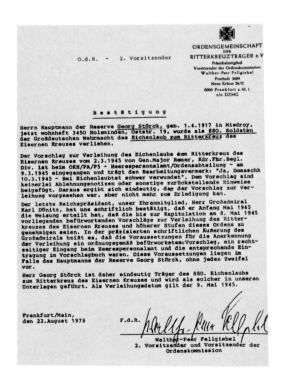

STURM, Hans-Hermann, First Lieutenant
3rd/Assault Brigade GD, Knight's Cross 6/9/1944
In an attack on the town of Parliti-Sat on April 4,
1944 First Lieutenant Sturm was able to destroy
numerous enemy tanks in fast moves and drive
the enemy infantry out of the town.

STÜTZLE, Nepomuk, Senior Corporal
Pz. Jäger Unit GD, Knight's Cross, 4/20/1945
Seven British tanks and numerous armored recon-
naissance cars were shot down by Senior Corporal
Stützle with his Panzerfaust at Nettelkamp and
Stadensen in the night of April 14-15, 1945.

382

	Hptm. Göbel, Kdr. II./G.R. 1226	27. 4. an OKH
Eichen- laub	Major v. Obstfelder, Kdr./Pz.Jg.Abt. 346	28. 4. an OKH
	Hptm. Methner, Kdr./II.Fallsch.A.R. 6	28. 4. an OKH
Eichen- laub	Gen.Lt. Plocher, Kdr./6.Fallsch.Jg.Div.	30. 4. an OKH
	Oberst Grosan, Kdr./Kampfgruppe Grosan	30. 4. an OKH
X	Lt. Anding, Adj./Pz.Jg.Abt.Groß- deutschld.	2. 5. an Führungs- stab A (FS)
X	Ogefr. Stützle, Pz.Jg.Abt. Groß- deutschld.	2. 5. an Führungs- stab A (FS.)
	Obstlt. Lier, Kdr. einer Kampfgruppe	2. 5. an Führungs- stab A
	Hptm. Lotze, Kampfgruppe Grosan	2. 5. an Führungs- stab A (FS.)

III.) Ich schlage trotzdem Verleihung durch den Großadmiral vor.

IV.) Ich verleihe den oben angeführten Soldaten die beantragten Auszeichnungen.

Großadmiral

V.) An Adjutantur der Wehrmacht beim Großadmiral.
MPA

14. Mai 1945 • Funkspruch an A.O.K. Ostpreußen

Nochmals Dank und Anerkennung für soldatische Haltung der Armee.
Verleihe Generalmajor Macher und 3 bewährten Angehörigen der 7. Inf.
Div. im Auftrage des Großadmirals das Ritterkreuz.

gez. Jodl

THIESSEN, Hans, Lieutenant
2nd/Anti-Aircraft Unit GD, Knight's Cross
5/9/1945
During action in the Bartenstein area between
February 10 and 18, 1945 Lieutenant Thiessen
and his 8.8 cm battery covered the German retreat
movement. When their ammunition ran out and
the enemy had already penetrated the gun
positions, the anti-aircraft gunners and their
young battery leader fought to the death, none
returning from their position alive.

TORNAU, Gottfried, Captain
Assault Artillery Brigade FGD, Knight's Cross
3/5/1945
While defending against enemy attacks from
February 16 to 18, 1945 the assault guns under
Captain Tornau made a determined countermove
toward Nantikow, stormed on to Liebenow and
were able to hold their position there.

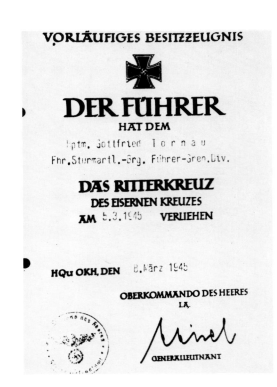

VOSHAGE, Werner, Major
Anti-Aircraft Unit BR, Knight's Cross 5/9/1945
In heavy defensive fighting in mid-April 1945 in the Spremberg-Weisswasser area, Major Voshage and his anti-aircraft unit repeatedly prevented breakthroughs by massive Soviet attacks near Wehrkirch, west of the Neisse.

WALLE, Gustav, Major
Pz. Jäger Unit GD, Knight's Cross 4/20/1945
In the hell of Stadensen-Nettelkamp on April 14-15, 1945, Major Walle destroyed nine British tanks with his Panzerfaust and stopped the attackers through his personal bravery. During this battle he was severely wounded.

WALTHER, Wilhelm, First Lieutenant
4./Construction Training Battalion zbV 800,
Knight's Cross 6/22/1940

First Lieutenant Walther was ordered to move
out ahead of the leading German attacking
troops with several commands of his company
and take possession of the undamaged Maas
bridge near Gennep. Before doing this, four
bridges over the Juliana Canal had to be taken,
which fell into German hands through camouflaged surprise attacks.

WANDREY, Max, Major
Jäger Regiment 1 BR, Knight's Cross 1/9/1944,
Oak leaves (787.) 3/16/1945

In bitter close combat against enemy bunkers on
the island of Leros in November of 1943, First
Lieutenant Wandrey and a shock troop stormed
forward and captured the British General Tilney
and his staff, who surrendered with the personnel
on the island. As the leader of a battle-march
battalion of Panzergrenadier Division Brandenburg, Major Wandrey had to deploy in-
experienced fighting men to free encircled groups
near Sprottisch-Waldau in mid-February 1944.
Thanks to his superior leadership, they were able
to fight their way out of the basin.

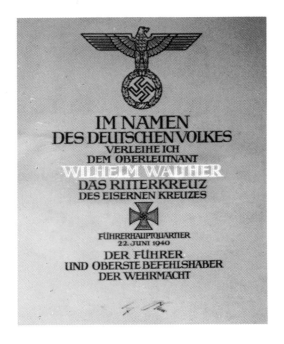

IM NAMEN
DES DEUTSCHEN VOLKES
VERLEIHE ICH
DEM OBERLEUTNANT
WILHELM WALTHER
DAS RITTERKREUZ
DES EISERNEN KREUZES

FÜHRERHAUPTQUARTIER
22. JUNI 1940
DER FÜHRER
UND OBERSTE BEFEHLSHABER
DER WEHRMACHT

WARSCHNAUER, Horst, Captain
Pz. Engineer Battalion GD, Knight's Cross
12/12/1942, oak leaves (753.) 2/24/1945

On September 22, 1942 First Lieutenant Warschnauer and his armored engineers stormed the town of Tschermassovo and, within 20 minutes, took more than 120 enemy bunkers. On his own initiative he stormed farther ahead and pursued the Soviets. Standing up in his SPW in February of 1945, Captain Warschnauer attacked the Russians in East Prussia, stormed enemy positions west of Brandenburg with his men in close combat, and thus covered the retreat to the west.

WATJEN, Rudolf, Major
Pz. Reconnaissance Unit GD, Knight's Cross
4/14/1943

Major Wätjen, as Commander of the GD Panzer Reconnaissance Unit, took a major role in the tank battle as Borissowka on March 14, 1943. By clever maneuvering, he lured the attacking enemy tanks before the guns of the GD Armored Regiment, which was able to destroy 21 of the attacking T-34 tanks.

Der Führer verlieh das Eichenlaub zum Ritterkreuz des Eisernen Kreuzes an Hauptmann Horst Warschnauer, Kommandeur unseres Sturmpionierbataillons.

DF. Unsere Sturmpioniere treten zum Gegenstoß an! Das brachte während der zurückliegenden schweren Kämpfe im ostpreußischen Raum oft die Entscheidung in schwierigsten Lagen. An der Spitze seiner Pioniere wagte Hauptmann Warschnauer wiederholt selbstständige Gegenstöße gegen starke gepanzerte Kräfte des Gegners.

Im Nahkampf unschlagbar—so nahmen sie M. im Sturm. Sie jagten dann die Sowjets von einer beherrschenden Höhe. Durch das erst auf kurze Entfernung eröffnete Abwehrfeuer der Bolschewisten blieb der Angriff zunächst liegen. In diesem Augenblick stieß der Kommandeur mit dem einzigen ihm zur Verfügung stehenden SPW vor. Aufrecht im Wagen stehend, riß er seine Männer mit lautem Hurra mit nach vorn und brach in den Feind ein. Seinen Männern mit Pistole und Handgranaten voranstürmend, wurden die Sowjets im Nahkampf erledigt und in kurzer Zeit die Höhe genommen. 170 Feindtote wurden gezählt.

Vorläufiges Besitzeugnis

Der Führer
und Oberste Befehlshaber
der Wehrmacht
hat

dem   Major Wätjen
         Kdr.A.A. "GD"

das Ritterkreuz
des Eisernen Kreuzes

am   14.4.1943   verliehen.

HQu OKH, den   15.April 1943

Das Oberkommando des Heeres
i.A.

Generalmajor

WEGNER, Wilhelm, Master Sergeant
1st/Assault Brigade GD, Knight's Cross
6/27/1943
Despite the crushing superiority of the Soviets at
Stanavoje on March 14, 1943, Master Sergeant
Wegner did not give up, but attacked the enemy
tanks from the flank. His personal success was
the destruction of six enemy tanks, clearing the
way for the armored reconnaissance unit.

WIETERSHEIM, Walter von, Captain
II./Pz. Regiment GD, Knight's Cross 5/15/1944
In the action near Jassy on March 7, 1944 Captain
von Wietersheim opened the way to further
success for the hard-fighting troops by destroying
14 enemy tanks, six antitank guns and two guns.

Knight's Cross, Oak Leaves and Swords awarded
Listed by date of awarding

	Name	Rank	Date	Pg.
Grossdeutschland	Garski, Eugen	Lt.Col.	7/19/40	194
	Beck-Broichsitter, Helmut	1st Lt.	9/4/40	185
	Hindelang, Hans	M.Sgt.	9/4/40	199
	Hänert, Karl	1st Lt.	8/2ì1	196
	Frantz, Peter	1st Lt.	6/4/42	193
	Greim, Alfred	Lt.Col.	6/4/42	196
	Blumenthal, Carl-Ludwig	1st Lt.	9/18/42	187
	Kohlhaas, Ludwig	Lt. Col.	11/21/42	205
	Klemm, Hans	Sergeant	12/10/42	203
	Warschnauer, Horst	1st Lt.	12/12/42	233
	Lorenz, Karl	Major	12/17/42	210
	Böhrendt, Max	1st Lt.	2/8/43	188
	Gehrke, Kurt	Lt.Col.	2/8/43	194
	Hoernlein, Walter (Oak 213)	Lt.Gen.	3/15/43	199
	Count Strachwitz von Gross Zauche und Camminetz, Hyazinth (Swords 27),	Colonel	3/28/43	228
	Magold, Hanns	1st Lt.	4/3/43	211
	Wätjen, Rudolf	Major	4/14/43	233
	Frantz, Peter (Oak 228)	Captain	4/14/43	193
	Pössl, Walter	Major	4/20/43	217
	Remer, Otto-Ernst	Major	5/18/43	219
	Wegner, Wilhelm	M.Sgt.	6/27/43	234
	Kahsnitz, Erich	Colonel	7/15/43	201
	Spaeter, Helmuth	Captain	7/28/43	223
	Konopka, Gerhard	1st Lt.	8/29/43	205
	von Natzmer, Oldwig	Lt. Col.	9/4/43	213
	Lex, Hans	1st Lt.	9/10/43	209
	Hückel, Ernst-Albrecht	Captain	9/27/43	200
	Herbst, Josef	1st Lt.	9/30/43	198
	Poschusta, Leopold	Sergeant	11/12/43	217
	Remer, Otto-Ernst (Oak 325)	Major	11/12/43	219
	Rampel, Josef	Sergeant	12/15/43	218
	Leyck, Siegfried	Captain	12/17/43	209
	Lorenz, Karl (Oak 395)	Colonel	2/12/44	210
	Kessel, Willi	M. Sgt.	2/23/44	202
	von Wietersheim, Walter	Captain	5/15/44	234
	Niemack, Horst (Swords 69)	Colonel	6/4/44	214
	Klemz, Bernhard	Captain	6/4/44	203
	Graf zu Rantzau, Hans-Friedrich	Captain	6/9/44	219
	Sturm, Hans-Hermann	1st Lt.	6/9/44	229
	Diddens, Diddo (Oak 501)	1st Lt.	6/15/44	229
	Schwarzrock, Rudolf	Major	8/19/44	227
	von Basse, Hans-Dieter	Major	9/10/44	185
	Sachs, Hans	Sr. Cpl.	9/10/44	222
	Röger, Hans	Sergeant	9/21/44	220
	Burg, Jörg(Oak 604)	1st Lt.	10/4/44	190
	Czorny, Wilhelm	Corporal	10/4/44	190
	Maaz, Heinz	Sr. Cpl.	10/4/44	210
	Graf von Rotkirch und Trach, Hans-Siegfried	Captain	10/4/44	221
	Bielig, Martin	M. Sgt.	10/7/44	186
	Larsen, Rudolf	Sergeant	10/23/44	207
	Rossmann, Emil	Lieut.	10/23/44	221
	Neumeyer, Werner	Lieut.	10/23/44	214
	Schroedter, Erich	Captain	10/23/44	226
	Bergmann, Heinz	M. Sgt.	11/26/44	186
	Plickat, Fritz	Sergeant	12/9/44	216
	Sommer, Clemens	Major	1/18/45	223
	Bock, Hans	Captain	2/5/45	187
	Heesemann, Wolfgang	Colonel	2/17/45	197
	Böhnk, Georg	1st Lt.	2/18/45	188
	Warschnauer, Horst (Oak 753)	Captain	2/24/45	233
	Pfau, Otto	Captain	3/23/45	183

	Kirsten, Rudi	Captain	3/28/45	202
	Schroedter, Erich (Oak 808)	Major	3/28/45	226
	Anding, Friedrich	Lieut.	4/20/45	184
	Stützle, Nepomuk	Sr. Cpl.	4/20/45	229
	Walle, Gustav	Major	4/20/45	231
	Paul, (first name unknown)	Sergeant	4/25/45	183
	Frankl, Adolf	Sergeant	4/26/45	183
	Fabich, Maximilian	Lt. Col.	5/8/45	191
	Thiessen, Hans	Lieut.	5/9/45	230
Brandenburg	Walther, Wilhelm	1st Lt.	6/22/40	232
	Grabert, Siegfried	1st Lt.	6/10/41	195
	von Foelkersam, Adrian	Lieut.	9/14/42	192
	Prohaska, Ernst	Lieut.	9/16/42	218
	Knaak, Hans-Wolfram	1st Lt.	11/3/42	204
	Lau, Werner	Lieut.	12/9/42	207
	Lange, Erhard	1st Lt.	1/15/43	206
	Oesterwitz, Karl-Heinz	1st Lt.	4/30/43	215
	von Koenen, Friedrich	Captain	9/16/43	204
	Grabert, Siegfried (Oak 320)	Captain	11/6/43	195
	Wandrey, Max	1st Lt.	1/9/44	232
	Steidl, Konrad	Captain	1/26/44	227
	Oesterwitz, Karl-Heinz (Oak 734)	Lt. Col.	2/10/45	215
	von Brückner, Erich	Colonel	3/11/45	189
	Wandrey, Max (Oak 787)	Major	3/16/45	232
	Afheldt, Eckart	1st Lt.	3/17/45	184
	Röseke, Erich	1st Lt.	4/8/45	222
	von Leipzig, Hellmut	Lieut.	4/28/45	208
	Bröckerhoff, Wilhelm	Major	5/8/45	189
	Müller-Rocholtz, Friedrich	Captain	5/8/45	213
	Voshage, Werner	Major	5/9/45	231
Kurmark	Riedmüller, Adam	Sergeant	2/8/45	220
	Schöne, Hans-Wolfgang	1st Lt.	3/23/45	225
Brigade von Werthern	Francois, Edmund	Captain	10/20/44	193
Führer Escort Battalion	Pohlmann, Wilhelm	Captain	3/14/43	216
	Famula, Günther	Lieut.	5/4/44	192
Führer Escort Brigade	von Möllendorff, Leonhard	Captain	1/8/45	212
	Scheunemann, Kurt	Sergeant	1/8/45	224
	Holm, Max	M. Sgt.	1/19/45	200
	Krieg, Gerhard	M. Sgt.	3/28/45	206
Führer Escort Division	Geisberg, Wilhelm	1st Lt.	4/14/45	195
	Fischer, Franz	Sergeant	4/30/45	183
	Schulte, Hubert	Captain	4/30/45	226
	Schnappauf, Georg	Lt. Col.	4/19/45	225
	Störck, Georg (Oak 880)	Captain	5/9/45	228
Führer Grenadier Brigade	Heinrich, Willi	Lieut.	12/9/44	197
	Lehnhoff, Ernst G.	Major	12/12/44	208
	Kapsreiter, Franz	M. Sgt.	1/14/45	201
Führer Grenadier Division	Hensel, Herbert	Captain	3/5/45	198
	Tornau, Gottfried	Captain	3/5/45	230
	Sommer, Ruprecht	Major	4/5/45	183
	Mäder, Hellmuth (Swords 143)	Maj. Gen.	4/18/45	211
	Klemt, Heinrich	Captain	5/2/45	183
	Matheja, Siegmund	Sergeant	5/6/45	212
	Nuhn, Heinrich	Captain	5/9/45	215
	Schmidt, E. (Oak 877)	Lt. Col.	5/9/45	224

The pictures and reproductions come from the soldiers, from German and other archives, and the GD photo archives.

Compiled by K.-H. Steffens, 3107 Hambühren, and Helmuth Spaeter, 8088 Eching a.A.

These pictures represent the many gatherings and other meetings: Days of memories, togetherness and unending comradeship!

Lieutenant General Hoernlein delivering the opening address in Lüneburg, 1953.

GD Association meeting in Arolsen, 1980.

Association meeting in Arolsen, 1981.

Association meeting in Radstadt/Tauern, Austria, 1982—The Citizen Guard.

Wreath for the fallen—

Cemetery in Arolsen, 1981.

Eternal lamp. given by the Tradition Association GD for the military cemetery at Oberwölbling, Austria, for 150 fallen GD soldiers in the St. Pölten-Krems area.

PHOTO CREDITS

N: Heirs   **GD-A.: GD Archives**   **KTB: War Record Books**

Page

142 GD-A., Kahler, Arnold (N), KB-Müller
143 Teusch, Waldow, von Werthern
144 GD-Manu 6, Hartmann
145 US Army, Signal Corps Photos-ETO-Hq. 44-3127 + SC 19 78 25-S
146 Blumenthal, Schönberg, KB-Müller
147 NFW 5//1975, Mäder
148 KB-Höpfner, Arnold (N), Frankfurter Illustrierte No. 14/July 1949
149 Hartmann, Arnold (N).
150 Hartmann
151 Scheunemann, Hartmann
152 GD-Manu 9, Waldow
153 GD-Bild-Archiv (11 x)
154 *Die Feuerwehr* no.20, Wackernagel
155 KB-Weidner
156 Wegener (2 x), Reichelt (2 x N)
157 Dr. Hölzer, KB-Weidner
158 GD-A., Märtens, KB-Weidner
159 Reichelt (N)
160 GD-Karten-Archiv, GD-A.
161 GD-A.
162 GD-A., Irlesberger

163 Gd-A. (2 x), Weihn.Brief 1.BR, Doerper (N), Golm
164 Doerper (N), Schmalbruch (N), Harms
165 Harms (3 x)
166 Schmalbruch (N), Töpelmann, von Aderkas
167 Dr. Jebens (3 x)
168 Schmalbruch (2 x), Irlesberger, GD-Karten-Archiv
169 Schmalbruch (N), GD-Karten-Archiv, Neumann
170 170GD-A, BA-Freiburg, von Werthern
171 Weih.Brief 1. BR (1981), Irlesberger
172 Weih.Brief 1. BR (1981), Dr. Hölzer, Brandt
173 Schafmeister, GD-Karten-Archiv
174 GD-Manu 8, KB-Müller, NFW No. 53/1953
175 Thiel, GD-Manu 8, von Brocke
176 Pietsch (2 x N), GD-Karten-Archiv
177 Pietsch (2 x N)
178 Pietsch (2 x N)
179 Lehnhoff (N), Hister, Kommission zu Berlin 1975 (Ausschnitt), Sommer
180 Pietsch (N), Hegrebe, GD-A.
181 NFW 157 (1965), Hogrebe
182 Niederstein, GD-A., Dusch

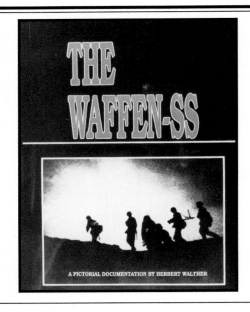
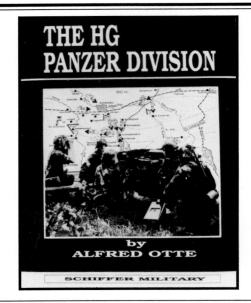